THEOLOGY, CHURCH AND MINISTRY

JOHN MACQUARRIE

Theology, Church and Ministry

CROSSROAD • NEW YORK

1986

The Crossroad Publishing Company
370 Lexington Avenue, New York, N.Y. 10017

©John Macquarrie 1986

Printed in the United States of America

Library of Congress Cataloging-in-Publication Data

Macquarrie, John.
   Theology, church, and ministry.

   Bibliography: p.
   1. Theology. 2. Church. 3. Christianity and other
religions. 4. Pastoral theology. I. Title
BT80.M32 1986   230'.3   86-9013
ISBN 0-8245-0787-8

To My Colleagues
Past and Present
in the Cathedral Church
of Christ in Oxford

Contents

Preface

This book gathers together a number of scattered papers which were written for various occasions and published in different journals and symposia. By a coincidence, it is exactly fifty years since I first began to read works in theology and religious thought, and the first chapter of the book traces developments in the theological world during those years and my own reactions to what has been going on.

The remaining chapters fall into three fairly well defined groups. The first group deals with various aspects of and approaches to theology as we confront it at the present time – theology and ideology (ch. 2), theology and empiricism (ch. 3), theology and biblical studies (ch. 4), theology and tradition (ch. 5), anthropology as a way into theology (ch. 6), the relative importance of experience and argument (ch. 7), the question of a theology of nature (ch. 8), and the question whether there is an Anglican theology, with reference to some recent discussions (ch. 9). Then there are five chapters on the church. The first of them asks whether there has not been an excessive disenchantment with the church and whether the time has come to seek to restore confidence (ch. 10), the next explores the notion of the church as 'people of God' and stresses the openness of this image in relation to those who are outside of the church (ch. 11), and the next three continue this theme by exploring a question in which I have long been interested – Christianity's relation to other faiths (ch. 12–14). Finally, there are four chapters on the ministry of the church. The first considers the nature of the ordained ministry (ch. 15), the remaining three take up somewhat controversial topics: the theological responsibilities of the bishop (ch. 16), the question of women priests (ch. 17) and the question of a political ministry (ch. 18).

I am grateful to those who first commissioned or published these papers, and my thanks is expressed in an acknowledgment at the end of the notes to each chapter.

Oxford, 1986   John Macquarrie

1

Pilgrimage in Theology

My theological pilgrimage began in 1936 when at Glasgow University I embarked on the long course of preparation for the ministry of the Church of Scotland. The seven years were divided into four that were spent on the rigorous course of study leading to the MA with honours in mental philosophy; and three on theology, leading to the BD.

Probably most theologians experience a tension in their work. I have known one from the beginning.

On the one hand, I had a naturally religious temperament. With me, 'religion' is not a bad word, as it was with Barth and many others. By 'religion' I mean an awareness of the holy, of the depth and mystery of existence. It can be a sense of presence, or, paradoxically, a sense of absence. Perhaps it is part of my Celtic heritage, for it is very close to the sense of presence which John Baillie described, and which he said he had had from the beginning of his life and which he took to be the main root of belief in God. Like Baillie too, I thought of this mystery in terms of immanence rather than transcendence. It was this kind of religious experience that drew me away from the rather dreary evangelical Protestantism in which I had been reared towards what may be broadly called the 'catholic' tradition – first as I found it within the 'High Kirk' movement in the Church of Scotland itself, especially at Govan Parish Church, and then beyond that in the Scottish Episcopal Church. But neither then nor later did I feel any urge to go to Rome. To begin with, the attraction was that of liturgy, forms of worship which through symbol and sacrament made real the presence of God in a way I had not experienced in services dominated by preaching. But I soon realized that liturgy cannot be isolated. It implies a whole complex of theology and spirituality and a distinctive way of understanding the church, so that one has really to buy the whole catholic package, so to speak.

But there came the problem, and I pass to the other side of the tension. My philosophical studies were immersing me in logic, ethics and epistemology. We studied many philosophers, ancient and modern, from Plato to Wittgenstein, whose *Tractatus* was beginning to have a vogue. But the one who really bowled me over was F. H. Bradley, whose *Principles of Logic* we had to study in considerable detail. I was deeply impressed by the vigour and clarity of his ideas. I went on to *Appearance and Reality*, and for several years that was my Bible, so to speak. 'Our orthodox theology on the one side and our commonplace materialism on the other,' wrote Bradley, 'vanish like ghosts before the daylight of free sceptical inquiry.'[1] I found his idea of the suprarational Absolute very congenial, and it obviously cohered rather well with my own somewhat pantheistic religiosity. I followed him too in his teaching that the doctrines of Christianity and its supposed historical basis are simply symbols (he did not use the word 'myth') of eternal truths. Like Kant and Hegel before him, he clearly believed that theological doctrines are at the best stages on the way to a higher philosophical truth.

With this background, the three years that I spent in the formal study of theology were not the happiest in my life! Biblical criticism and church history I found interesting, and we did a limited amount of philosophy of religion, but dogmatic theology I had come to regard as little more than systematic superstition. Calvin and Barth (who was the big name at that time) I found specially insufferable. Theories of atonement and incarnation seemed to me a waste of time. If *The Myth of God Incarnate* had come out at that time, I would have swallowed it whole! Still, there were some crumbs of comfort. *The Idea of the Holy,* by Rudolf Otto, made a strong appeal; and while I had little use for the lectures of Dr Gossip when he was on his own subject of pastoral theology, I found fascinating a course which he gave on Buddhism – he was one of the few people in this country to have mastered the Pali language and to have studied the Buddhist scriptures in the original. At the end of the three years, I was offered a scholarship to go to Cambridge to do graduate studies in theology at Westminster College. I politely declined, and for the next seven years I never opened a book of theology.

These seven years were spent in the pastoral ministry, first as an Army chaplain and then in a parish in the northeast of Scotland. I had worked out a *modus vivendi*, but not on any definite theological basis. My return to theology was almost accidental. One of my former theology professors, Dr J. G. Riddell, was vacationing near my parish and came to see me. It was kind of him to do so, seeing I had been such a pain in the neck as a student! In the course of his visit, he asked if I had ever thought of taking up the further studies which I had earlier declined. He mentioned that he had a brilliant new colleague, Professor Ian Henderson, working on Bultmann, and thought that my parish duties were light enough to allow me to do research and to travel occasionally to Glasgow for supervision. The upshot was that I began working for a PhD, the thesis topic being the influence of Heidegger's philosophy upon Bultmann's theology. My supervisor was Ian Henderson, and it would be impossible to think of a better one. His mind was both profound and acutely critical, and my theological pilgrimage owes more than I can express to his guidance and stimulation.

The thesis resulting from this research became my first book, *An Existentialist Theology* (1955). It sought to show how Bultmann's interpretation of the New Testament as a way of life had drawn upon the analysis of human existence given by Heidegger, and Bultmann himself was kind enough to commend the work as an accurate presentation of his thought. Its importance for my own pilgrimage was that, although it was not uncritical of Bultmann, it did seem to me to bring me much closer to reconciling religious faith with intellectual integrity than had been possible while Bradley's philosophy still held sway in my mind. I explicitly contrasted Bradley and Bultmann in these words: '[Bradley's] view is poles apart from Bultmann's. The idealist identifies the essence of Christianity with a high philosophy of the universe, but for Bultmann Christianity is a religion with saving power. For the idealist, the mighty acts become mere optional symbols of suprarational truth, but for Bultmann they constitute God's unique act of grace. For the idealist, the significance of these acts for the individual is a purely intellectual one, but for Bultmann they summon to a decision, in so far as they present a possibility of existence.'[2] In the meantime I had become Lecturer in Systematic Theology at Glasgow University (I no longer called it 'systematic superstition'!) and for the next ten years or so, stretching into my time at Union Theological Seminary, New York, where I went in 1962, I was in my 'existentialist' phase. The books reflecting this, as well as the one I have mentioned, were *The Scope of Demythologizing* (1960) and a volume of collected essays, *Studies in Christian Existentialism* (1965). In addition, I spent many weary hours, in collaboration with Edward Robinson, in translating Heidegger's massive and difficult *Being and Time* (1962).

I was never, however, quite happy with Bultmann's almost pure existentialism. It seemed to me in danger of becoming quite subjective. I noted too that although Bultmann relied heavily on the earlier Heidegger, he took no notice of the later ontological work. I felt that I had to broaden the base of my theology. Tillich's *Systematic Theology*, which had begun to appear in 1953, attracted me, though I think that most of what is of value in its philosophical structure has been better said by Heidegger. But more important than Tillich was my discovery of Rahner, who at that time was untranslated and virtually unknown in Britain. The first thing of his that I read was his little work on death. He had been a student of Heidegger, but he takes up the study of death where Heidegger leaves off, and the result seemed to me to be that synthesis of catholic faith and philosophical thought for which I had been searching. I eagerly read other works of his, and found his writings on christology especially illuminating. Hans Urs von Balthasar was another Catholic writer whom I came across about that time. Incidentally, my discovery of these two writers came about while I was gathering material for my *Twentieth-Century Religious Thought* (1963). That survey, which expanded far beyond what I had originally envisaged, was in part due to my desire to break out of a narrow existentialism and, as I said in the Preface, even if no one else were to benefit from it, I would have educated myself in the writing of it.

Soon after I went to the United States, several events occurred which had a bearing on my theological thinking.

First, I decided that the time had come to identify myself with the Anglican communion. I had been flirting with the Episcopal Church long enough, though it would take too long to explain here why I had not joined it many years before. But now the way was clear, and in 1965 I was ordained in January to the diaconate and in June to the priesthood by Bishop Donegan of New York. Although the decision was entirely my own and had been contemplated for a long time, I was encouraged in this transition by a new friendship which I had formed with John Knox, the renowned New Testament scholar. A few days after our arrival in New York, he had put in my mailbox a copy of his latest book, *The Church and the Reality of Christ*. His New Testament scholarship was no less radical than Bultmann's, but he combined it with a very high view of the church – indeed, in his theology Christ and the church comprise together the unity of the Christ-event. I owe much not only to his writings but to his friendship and many conversations. John Knox, already into his sixties, was at that time himself seeking ordination in the Episcopal Church and it seemed natural to me to follow his example. I think we both felt that it was important to *practise* the kind of religious faith that we were expounding in our teaching, for theology without corresponding practice is surely empty. I should add, however, that in becoming an Anglican, I did not feel that I was renouncing my past. Rather, I was taking it with me into something broader, richer, more fulfilling, more catholic. I am glad to see that Louis Bouyer has understandingly written about me that 'Beginning from Bultmann, for whom he had a great admiration, he has developed towards positions which, without denying anything that is positive in the protestant tradition, approach closely to the catholic vision.'[3]

A second important event from this time was an invitation from Charles Scribner's Sons, the New York publishers, to write a one-volume systematic theology. The result was my *Principles of Christian Theology* (1966). This book, I hope, though it set out from man's existential situation, broke out of narrow existentialism and treated the theme in what I called clumsily enough the 'existential-ontological' manner, while it also reflected my Anglican orientation in its treatment of church and sacraments. Eric Mascall, a severe critic of existentialism, reviewed the book generously, and agreed that the usual criticisms of existentialism did not affect it. Perhaps the most criticized part was the doctrine of God. Several critics held that it came near to pantheism. No doubt it reflected my early religiosity, and perhaps Bradley's suprarational Absolute was still lurking there in the new guise of Heidegger's Being. Nevertheless, at that time this book was the closest I could come to the synthesis of catholic faith and a reasonable philosophy.

A third event of those years was the outbreak of controversy over God – Bishop Robinson's *Honest to God*, then the various forms of 'death of God' theology, put forward by van Buren, Hamilton, Altizer and others, to say nothing of the 'secular' Christianity and 'religionless' Christianity advocated by Harvey Cox and various would-be interpreters of Bonhoeffer. As far as Bishop Robinson's speculations were concerned, I felt that his 'panentheism' was very close to my own position, and immediately sent him a copy of my inaugural lecture at Union. But the reader can readily believe that 'death of God' and 'religionless Christianity' were movements which I felt had to be resisted at all costs. In 1967 I produced two books in which I entered into controversy with these views. One was *God-Talk*, which has turned out to be one of my most influential books and has been translated into several languages. The other was *God and Secularity*. This second book marks, I think, a turning point in my development. In my earlier writings, I think I was usually on the side of the liberals. But now, it seemed to me, the faith was being so much reduced and humanized that it was necessary to take a stand on the central beliefs of traditional Christianity. The same spirit animated my *Paths in Spirituality* (1972). A reviewer in *The Scotsman*, welcoming the defence that I offered of prayer and religious practices, said that it came from 'a man frightened by the emptiness he saw looming up in the "New Theology" ', and I would not quarrel with that judgment.

Meanwhile I had returned to this country to become Lady Margaret Professor of Divinity at Oxford in 1970. The chair is linked to a canonry of Christ Church, so I now found myself in the ideal position of doing theology in the context of the daily office and the daily eucharist. Most of the books I have written since coming to Oxford are expansions of topics that could be treated only briefly in my *Principles*. Thus *Three Issues in Ethics* (1970) and *The Concept of Peace* (1973) develop further the question of the Christian's conduct in the world. *Christian Hope* (1978) enlarges on the eschatological themes. Engagement in ecumenical discussion led to *Christian Unity and Christian Diversity* (1975), a book which – again in agreement with John Knox – stresses the central role of Rome in the drawing together of the churches, and visualizes also a form of unity which will not stifle pluralism and legitimate diversity. *Thinking about God* (1975) and *The Humility of God* (1978) return to the God question, and seek to clarify and deepen my earlier teaching on the subject. The second of these books, though very small and put together in a hurry to help a publisher who had been inadvertently let down at a critical moment, does represent a development in my thinking, for while it speaks of God's immanence and down-to-earthness, as do my previous writings, it links this far more definitely with the idea of incarnation. That the church needs a theologically educated laity has always been a conviction of mine, and *The Faith of the People of God* (1972) was a contribution to that end. It has been impossible to keep up with developments in philosophy, but I am glad that I have written books that are philosophical rather than theological – a short one on *Martin Heidegger* (1968) and a longer one on *Existentialism* (1972). The latter, in the form of a Pelican, has reached a very wide non-theological readership.

In 1977 I produced a revised and enlarged edition of the *Principles of Christian Theology*. This was meant to take account of criticisms, to note important contributions by theologians who had appeared on the scene since the first edition was written, and to reflect changes in my own thinking. I can mention only a few of the changes. There is a more affirmative attitude to the traditional natural theology, due in the main to reading Basil Mitchell's writings. In the treatment of human existence, there is less stress on finitude and more on the inborn human drive to transcendence. The statements about God have been carefully reviewed, and I have used the expression 'panentheism' to describe my position. There is much new material on christology, and especially a discussion of the definitiveness of Jesus Christ for Christians amid the competing claims of the world religions. There is considerable fresh material too on the Holy Spirit, for the charismatic movement has made it imperative that we should clear up our ideas about the Spirit. Whereas in the first edition I had said that the infallibility of the Pope is an insuperable barrier to union with Rome, my experience of ecumenical discussion and particularly some exchanges with Bishop B. C. Butler have led me to put things rather differently. These are only a few of the more obvious changes, but I hope they show that the pilgrimage continues!

What of the future? It has been my contention for a long time that the doctrine of man is the right starting point for a contemporary theology, and this belief led me in the late 1970s to work on a study of the human condition from a Christian viewpoint. There are many difficulties in such a study, such as the limitations of one's own knowledge and experience and the problem of finding the most effective order in which to present and relate to one another the many facets of the human phenomenon. I worked by the method of giving lectures on various aspects of the human being – such as freedom, transcendence, alienation and so on – eventually bringing these into a unified study which was published in 1982 with the title, *In Search of Humanity*. In the meanwhile, an invitation to give the Gifford Lectures at St Andrews University gave me the idea of writing a companion volume, *In Search of Deity*, published in 1984. In this book I took up an even more affirmative attitude to natural theology and, I hope, considerably clarified my conception of God, as several critics had claimed that this was not at all clear in my earlier writings. But to have written on humanity and deity, themes which are both necessary prolegomena to the study of christology, is to suggest that I complete a trilogy with a volume on the God-man. I have written at least a dozen articles on christology and have thought that some time I would like to attempt a systematic study, but have never felt quite ready. But if the riches of Christ are 'unsearchable', what would it mean to be ready? The life of the theologian will always be a pilgrimage with no stopping place that he or she can consider final. In what time remains to me, I shall carry on my quest for a Christian theology truly catholic and truly critical.

2

Theology and Ideology

Since the time of the Enlightenment, the West has been very much captivated by a certain ideal of knowledge. The adjectives 'objective' and 'value-free' have been used to describe this ideal of knowledge. These adjectives indicate that it is to be purified of all 'subjective' influences and that it is to stick to facts, disregarding any value-judgments upon them. This also implies an investigator who is 'detached' from and 'uninvolved' with the subject matter, an investigator who is a pure observer of phenomena. Indeed, if possible, it would be desirable to replace the human observer by some impersonal equipment. These requirements have led in course of time to the development of the empiricist theory of knowledge. From universally observable phenomena one is supposed to proceed by universally accepted logical methods of induction to universally accepted generalizations.

But this ideal has nowadays been more and more called into question. On the one hand, some philosophers of science have criticized the logic of induction, and have argued that imagination plays just as important a part in scientific discovery as does observation, and that in any case the scientist is never the passive recipient of objective data but is already selecting and evaluating the phenomena. Karl Popper boldly declares, 'There can be no pure observational language, since all languages are impregnated with theories and myths.'[1] On the other hand, a different group of philosophers has been arguing that all knowledge has an inescapable personal dimension. Into every act of knowing there enters, albeit tacitly, something of the interests and values of the knower. Michael Polanyi has been the best known exponent of this view in Britain. He goes so far as to say that 'any attempt rigorously to exclude our human perspective from our picture of the world must lead to absurdity'.[2]

The 'value-free' ideal itself implies a value-system, for which, in its own terms, it can offer no justification. If it had any plausibility at all, this would be only in the most formal and abstract subjects, such as mathematics and physics. This helps to explain why Descartes and his successors prized mathematics above all other sciences, and tried to assimilate all knowledge to the mathematical ideal. Spinoza tried to treat ethics by the methods of geometry, and nearer our own time Carnap envisaged in his concept of 'physicalism' the reduction of all sciences to the language of physics. Such attempts surely do merit the charge of absurdity. Today there would be much more sympathy than formerly for the belief that each science has its own appropriate methodology, and that in varying degrees the interests and values of the investigator will enter into his work. Even the mathematician derives satisfaction from the aesthetic elegance of his demonstrations.

Let us turn from these general considerations to the special question of religion and theology. Here we may note that the Oxford Theology Honour School, when founded in the nineteenth century, was designed to conform to the objective and value-free ideals that were influential at that time. This accounts for the heavily biblical and historical orientation of the school. One could hardly teach or examine anyone on the subjects of, say, God or the eucharist – that would be to stray into the realms of private subjective opinion, so it was supposed. The attitude was reinforced by the acute denominational sensitivities prevailing in those days. But it was all right, let us say, to teach and examine Anselm's doctrine of God or Ratramnus' teaching about the eucharist. These are matters of ascertainable fact, and at least in theory they can be objectively taught and objectively examined. This traditional attitude helps to explain why England has been weak in systematic theology but strong in historical theology. A few years ago, a move was made to reduce the historical bias in the Oxford Honour School, and to allow more room to systematic theology. The move was defeated by a coalition of those who believe that, in order to be academically respectable, theology may deal only with the question of who said what, not with the substantive questions of religious truth themselves. When a much more modest change in the curriculum was introduced to replace the defeated scheme, I myself heard someone say in the discussion: 'You mustn't pry into a person's private beliefs!'

Of course, there is a difference between theology and religious belief. The difference is twofold. A religious belief has a measure of naiveté about it. It is confessional language, evoked by some powerful impression made on the believer. Examples would be the confessions of the apostles Peter and Thomas recorded in the New Testament expressing their response to Jesus of Nazareth. 'You are the Christ!' says Peter (Mark 8.29). 'My Lord and my God,' says Thomas (John 20.28). Theology is a second-order language, and therefore more sophisticated, more critical and more reflective. The theologian might begin from confessions of faith, like the two quoted, but he then inquires about the meaning of the terms used, such as 'Christ' and 'Lord' and 'God', he inquires further about the implications of these terms, their coherence, the reasons that led to their being applied to Jesus, and so on. In this way he may come to develop a complete christology. The second element in the twofold difference concerns the mode of assent. If we may use Newman's terminology, a religious belief calls for real assent. Peter and Thomas were committing themselves to Jesus Christ in a fairly total way, and it was certainly more than an intellectual act. They were taking up an existential stance. But when one begins to theologize, reflectively and critically, one has, so to speak, taken a step back. Sometimes, of course, a theological belief may be passionately held. One can readily suppose, for instance, that in eucharistic controversies some have given real assent to such difficult doctrines as transubstantiation and consubstantiation. However, one may also suppose that a real assent could be given to the religious belief, in this case belief in a real presence of Christ, but only a notional or even a modified assent to the theological interpretation.

If one accepts that there is the twofold difference just described between religious belief and theology, then this throws some light on the question whether someone who is not a believer could either study or teach theology. It seems to me that one could neither teach a subject nor study it with any seriousness unless one believed that it had some integrity and value. Thus, if someone supposed that the subject-matter of theology is non-existent or illusory, he could hardly be a serious student of theology or a teacher of theology. He might, of course, be a good student of philosophy of religion, trying to present a theory of religion as illusion, though I think some philosophers of religion would question this. But I would say that an atheist could not be a serious student or teacher of Christian theology. On the other hand, I would hesitate to say the same about an agnostic. An agnostic is unable to give real assent to first-order religious beliefs, but he might have sufficient sympathy with them to take seriously the interpretations of these beliefs as found in the second-order language of theology, and to teach theology effectively and conscientiously as a serious subject.

I have criticized the notion of a detached or value-free study of religion and theology, and claimed that some minimal sympathy must be present. This does not mean for one moment, however, that the only alternative to the value-free approach is some form of subjectivism or propaganda. In modern totalitarian states, the socio-political ideology of such a state or even a complete philosophy of life is propagated with all the resources of the educational system and the various media. Perhaps religion could be propagated in such a way also, and no doubt it has sometimes been so propagated. But, certainly from the Christian point of view, such a propagation of religion would be self-defeating. For Christianity has as one of its basic teachings respect for the human person, and this kind of propaganda is a manifest disregard for the person, who is seen as an object to be manipulated.

Equally, such an activity is an offence against any educational theory that respects personal integrity.

Leaving aside the question of propaganda, it is even
doubtful if Christian teaching should take the form of apologetics, that is to say, a form in which it is presented as
superior to alternative beliefs. If this were to be done without
falling into mere propaganda, then one would need to be
very careful to state clearly and give a fair hearing to the
alternative viewpoints and their objections to Christian
belief. So often the apologist presents the alternatives in
some weak or implausible form, so that one suspects he is
setting up a straw man with the sole purpose of demolishing
it. Karl Popper truly remarks that 'there is no point in
discussing or criticizing a theory unless we try all the time
to put it in its strongest form, and to argue against it only in
that form'.[3] A common error is to present some generalized
argument and then to show its weakness. But I think one has
to be concrete, and face the actual objections and criticisms
of major atheistic thinkers, such as Feuerbach, Marx,
Nietzsche, Freud, Sartre and others.

But even if one seeks to be as fair as possible in such
an apologetic presentation of Christianity, some theologians
would still believe that a controversial statement of this kind
is unsatisfactory. They would say that the best defence of
Christian faith is simply to say what it is, to let it be seen in
its own light, so to speak, without engaging in polemics.
Apologetic arguments for the reasonableness or superiority
of Christian belief have their place only or chiefly when
doubts and questions arise, either in our own minds or in
the minds of those whom we are addressing.

I have mentioned socio-political philosophies that are
sometimes propagated in totalitarian states, and what I had
in mind were, for instance, Fascism, Nazism, Marxism,
Maoism and the like. These have become substitute religions
in our time, and they are believed and preached with all the
fervour of a religious fanatic. They are sometimes called
'ideologies'. Actually, this word 'ideology' has several meanings, and I do not believe that this one is the most important.
In any case, we have seen that Christianity could not become

an ideology in this sense without self-contradiction. It would be a bogus form of Christianity that sought to propagate itself with all the modern techniques of persuasion without any respect for the reason and conscience of the persons concerned.

The word 'ideology' has nowadays become a term of reproach. It is surely an irony that when we hear it, we associate it with some totalitarian socio-political doctrine, more likely than not with Marxism. This is an irony because Marx too used this term as one of reproach or even abuse, but presumably he did not dream that it would be applied to his own theories. In 1846, along with Engels, he wrote a work called *German Ideology*. Here the word is used in its distinctively Marxist sense to mean the beliefs and theories that are produced by the economic conditions of society. Marx believed that philosophies which claim to be products of pure reason are in fact expressions of class interest. If one carried this view to extreme lengths, obviously it would lead to a self-destroying scepticism. Yet we can have little doubt that, as against the Enlightenment glorification of reason, Marx was correct in claiming that interest enters into all our thinking. 'Ideology', in this sense, is something subtler and more important than ideology in the popular sense of a consciously propagated socio-political philosophy. In this other, Marxist, sense, ideology is an unconscious distortion of thought, derived from the influence of class interests. Marx himself believed that only the proletariat is free of ideology and has a clear vision of things as they really are, and so he sought to escape from the slide into scepticism.

Marx's own view of ideology has been criticized at many points, especially his attempt to derive it solely from economic class interest, and to exempt one class from its influence. But the residual truth in his view has been developed by later philosophers of neo-Marxist tendency, especially by Habermas in his book *Knowledge and Interest*. He broadens the range of the idea of interest to include more than economic factors, criticizes Kant and other philosophers who have believed that one can aspire to a wholly rational understanding of the world, but avoids a thoroughgoing scepticism by holding that through self-reflection and self-criticism we can overcome the worse effects of the interest which inevitably enters into our knowledge. Rather similar views are to be found in another neo-Marxist, Marcuse. He argues that even science and technology are by no means neutral or value-free. They are already impregnated with a consumption-oriented value system, which is hostile to the development of a free society. But he also believes that these false values can be overcome by critical reason.

It seems to me that one of the major challenges to theology today and to its teachers is to face the question of the relation of theology to ideology, in the sense in which this latter term is used by Marxists and neo-Marxists. We have seen that Christian theology is not, and cannot be, an ideology in the popular sense of the term – at least, if it ever became such, it would have destroyed itself. But is there perhaps an admixture of ideology in theology, in the more subtle Marxist sense of the term? Is it possible indeed to avoid it? Let me give a very simple example. For centuries the clergy of the Church of England were recruited almost exclusively from the two ancient universities of Oxford and Cambridge with their upper-class backgrounds. Was it not inevitable that this should have affected, even if unconsciously, their way of presenting Christianity, causing them to emphasize those elements which agreed with their interests, and to play down other elements that were less comfortable? Could this explain in part the alienation of the industrial masses from the church? Does it not also explain in part the Oxford Honour School of Theology, for that supposedly objective and value-free study of theology itself reflects a very definite scheme of value, that of the leisured intellectual?

It seems to me further that the challenge of ideology is making itself felt very sharply in the theological world today. For centuries, Christian theology was the almost exclusive preserve of a well-defined segment of the human race. Theologians were Europeans, and later North Americans; they worked in universities and were steeped in the traditions of Western, especially classical, learning; they were of middle-class or upper-class background; they were almost entirely of the male sex. Can it be seriously denied that this long association of theology with this segment of society has led to the infiltration into theology of ideas and values that derive from this social and cultural background, and have no basis in Christianity itself? While, conversely, other elements in the Christian message may have been unconsciously suppressed? At any rate, we seem to have come to a crisis, when hitherto silent and inarticulate groups are demanding that they too should have a share in shaping theology.

Let me mention four such groups.

In India, China, Africa and the Caribbean, there is a demand for what has become known as indigenous theology, that is to say, theology expressed in the images and concepts current in these cultures, in place of what to them are the alien concepts and images of the West. Indigenous theology was one of the leading items on the agenda of the world-wide Anglican Consultative Council of 1976, and already much has been achieved in both theology and liturgy in the matter of breaking out of Western moulds and using indigenous resources.

In the United States, although the black section of the population has always been profoundly religious, it has had until recently very little influence in theology or in the ethos of the main-line denominations. But now black theology has made its appearance, a type of theology which tries to understand Christianity in terms of the black experience. For this theology, Christ is black – not literally, for no one knows what his complexion was, but in the important sense that he is identified with the black experience.

In South America, where ever since independence was gained from the former Spanish and Portuguese rulers, there has been in most of the republics an almost unbroken series of tyrannous regimes, whether of the right or the left, now we hear of 'liberation theology', a theology which is conceived in terms of the concrete situation of these nations. For them, abstract Oxbridge debates on 'the myth of God incarnate' would be a meaningless and irrelevant exercise in theology. They are interested in what Christianity has to say about social justice and the liberation of the oppressed.

The last group I want to mention is not a minority group, like those already cited, but half the human race, namely, women. Though women have been active in the church from the beginning, and have provided their fair share of saints, martyrs and mystics, they have until recently been virtually excluded from theology. Is there not at least a strong probability that the monarchical, masculine, dominating concept of God, against which many people have rebelled in modern times, has been in part due to the male monopoly of theology, and the unconscious interests and prejudices which thus found their way into theology? Certainly, many of the new breed of women theologians believe that this has been the case, and are determined to let a different way of expressing matters be heard.

But will not this proliferation of different theologies, each seeing things from a distinctive viewpoint, each penetrated by special interests and a special ideology, have an utterly fragmenting effect, so that Christian theology will disappear in a mass of partial and often distorted points of view? I do not think so. There never will be one all-embracing theology, expressing in proper proportion all the truths of Christian faith. Certainly, our traditional Western theologies could not claim to have done that. They too were infected by ideology, just as much as black theology or liberation theology, though we were for the most part unaware of it and perhaps thought that Thomas Aquinas or Luther or Calvin was the universal voice of Christianity. But to deny that there will ever be an adequate all-embracing theology is not to resign oneself to sheer fragmentation or pluralism. Certainly, value-free theology is a chimera. No theology is free from ideological value-judgments. But a global theology is still possible, and is indeed a necessity for our shrinking world. I mean, a theology that would honestly admit the legitimacy of different interests and would encourage their expression. It would not try to harmonize them all in one inclusive statement, but would let them correct and enrich one another.

To sum up: theology, like other intellectual disciplines, is never value-free. To some extent, it will always embody the interests and valuations of the theologian. It is therefore never free from ideology, but the distorting effects of ideology can be minimized by encouraging theologians to work from different social and cultural backgrounds, to become as far as possible aware of these and critical of them, and to allow their findings to correct each other dialectically.

3

The End of Empiricism?

I suppose the title of this chapter must sound pretty shocking to most practitioners of philosophy in the English-speaking countries at the present time, even though I have put a question mark after it. For surely empiricism has acquired the status of something like a philosophical establishment? The first distinctively Anglo-Saxon philosophy was empiricist, represented by such outstanding thinkers as Locke, Berkeley and Hume. Along the way, empiricism has brought forth vigorous children, such as utilitarianism in England and pragmatism in the United States. Admittedly, for a generation or so the reign of empiricism was interrupted by the unaccountable rise of idealism, represented in England by Green, Caird, Bradley, Bosanquet and many others, and in America by Howison and Royce. But that proved to be only an episode. Soon empiricism was back in command again – indeed, in the extreme form popularized by Ayer, it took us all the way back to Hume. Perhaps it had been forgotten that Hume eventually gave up philosophy for backgammon.

It is hard to explain how philosophical fashions come and go. It is not necessary for a philosophy to be refuted – indeed, a philosophy is such a complex and intricate fabric of ideas that I doubt if any major type of philosophy could be finally refuted. There are always some elements of truth that will survive and some possibilities of reconstruction that will persist. Yet sometimes the life seems to have departed and there is no longer any spirit of creativity.

Let us suppose I had been sitting here in Oxford at the beginning of the century, rather than near its close. I would have been surrounded by idealist philosophers, many of them of the highest ability. The name of Hegel was much revered, even if his teaching was not always well understood. Many of the philosophers of that time spoke with a confidence and even a kind of finality, as if the end of the road had been reached. Could I have supposed for a moment that within two or three decades idealism would have virtually disappeared from the scene? I would not have had the perspicuity to foresee that, but a shrewd American, George Santayana, was able to read the signs of the times. In 1913 he wrote: 'Nothing will have been disproved, but everything will have been abandoned.'[1]

I suspect we may have come to another time of change in the philosophical climate. Empiricism has not been disproved but it has become tired and is creaking at the joints. It no longer commands the almost unquestioning assent that it enjoyed for so many years.

Of course, one has to make a number of discriminations. For instance, one has to distinguish between a narrower and a broader type of empiricism. Among the great names of empiricism, that of Locke has represented the broader type, that of Hume the narrower. Ayer's famous *Language, Truth and Logic* appeared exactly fifty years ago, in the same year that I began the study of theology. This initiated a period when the narrower empiricism, known as logical positivism, was the dominant philosophy in the English-speaking universities and it was against this background that I have had to do most of my theological work. We often hear nowadays that logical positivism is dead, and though this may be an exaggeration, I believe it has been largely discredited because of its own internal incoherences. The broader empiricism differs from the narrower variety chiefly in its willingness to acknowledge other kinds of experience as well as sense-experience – perhaps self-experience, interpersonal experience, aesthetic experience, even religious experience. But when one has opened the door to such a wide range of experiences and is willing to accord to all of them at least a *prima facie* recognition, the concept of empiricism begins to lose definition and may become so broad as to be quite misleading. One has also to distinguish between those limited areas where empiricism has proved its worth as a method of inquiry and the attempts to extend it to other areas where it may be much less successful, or even to turn it into a universal philosophy. Obviously, empiricism has had its greatest successes in the natural sciences. It was the empirical approach that chiefly differentiated modern science from that of the ancient Greeks, and that has accounted for the staggering growth of modern science. But when empirical methods are applied to the phenomena of human life, their usefulness turns out to be much more limited. No one can deny some value to psychology, sociology and kindred sciences, but they are able to deal with only those aspects of human life that are amenable to observation, experiment, quantification and so on. Those who favour other approaches complain, with good reason, that the empiricist misses out what is most distinctively human in his account. The existentialist, for instance, sees the essentially human in freedom and the possibility for transcendence, and empiricism has no way of dealing with these. The Marxist has a different criticism. Ernst Bloch, for instance, talks about 'crawling' empiricism, and he uses this uncomplimentary adjective because empiricism seeks to describe things as they are, but offers no criticism of what it describes nor any imaginative proposals for the betterment of our lot in this world. It offends against the Marxist principle that the business of the philosopher is not just to describe the world, but to change it.

It may be admitted that some of these criticisms of empiricism have been carried to exaggerated lengths. I have already conceded that in the field of natural science, empiricism has made a unique contribution. Even in the human sciences, empirical studies should not be ignored or neglected. The Marxist may be right in castigating a 'crawling' empiricism which merely describes the existing state of affairs, but his own proposals for a better order may turn out to be an empty utopianism (like Bloch's own philosophy) if it is not firmly anchored somewhere in empirical fact. As I have already indicated, when one speaks of the 'end of empiricism', one cannot mean its radical elimination, but simply cutting it back to its proper sphere and refuting its pretensions to be a universally applicable philosophy – virtually a metaphysic, however much the empiricist may dislike that word.

But, strange to say, some of the most damaging criticisms of empiricism have come not from existentialists or Marxists but from philosophers of science. It is precisely in the area where it is most firmly entrenched that questions about the claims of empiricism have arisen. Already in this book I have mentioned some of the questions raised by Popper and Polanyi.[2] Is there any pure observation that is not already coloured by theories, or even myths? Is it possible for any knower to be 'value-free', for does not his very selection of data depend on his judgment of what is significant and what is not? Is there not a personal dimension in every act of cognition? And there are many other critical questions that may be directed to the empiricist. How does it stand nowadays with the methods of inductive logic? Is there a sure way of proceeding from the observation of particular events to the formulation of general laws of nature? Is the thinking subject whom the empiricist sets over against a world of objects not a mere abstraction from a human being who participates in the full range of personal and social life? Can all worthwhile knowledge be put into propositional form and given clear conceptual expression, or is there not also a kind of knowledge which is very important but which cannot be said clearly? Following from this, we may ask further whether knowledge of facts is the basic form of knowledge, and whether it has a privileged status, as the empiricist seems to suppose.[3]

Up till now I have been talking about empiricism in general and showing how it is faltering at the present time, so that its dominance in Anglo-Saxon philosophy may be coming to an end. Let me now be more specific and consider the question of empiricism when applied to problems of theology and the philosophy of religion. Especially in the United States, there has for many decades been an attempt to develop empiricist philosophies of religion and even empiricist theologies. No doubt this has been an apologetic response to the empiricist temper of the times. Clearly, too, if any affirmative account of religion in empiricist terms is to be given, it would call for one of the broader forms of empiricism. The narrower forms seem inevitably to lead to negative evaluations of religious belief, and I shall have something to say about this later. I believe, however, that philosophies of religion when based on empiricism, even when they purport to be affirmative, share the weaknesses of empiricist philosophies in general. But I should say again that one cannot make a sweeping judgment, for every philosophical approach is likely to have some merits to offset its deficiencies and blind spots.

As long ago as 1945, James Alfred Martin wrote a book in which he examined some American empiricist philosophies of religion.[4] In this book he reviewed the work of five religious thinkers, each of whom could be considered an empiricist. Martin noted three characteristics which, more or less overtly, occurred in each of them and constituted their claim to be empiricists. In his own words, 'Each of our philosophers seeks to take a broadly "realistic" attitude toward the problems of religion. Each would base his religious views upon the "facts of experience", either experience in general or some form of religious experience in particular. And each would establish his conclusions through an appeal to some form of empirical method.'[5]

Martin's studies are notable for the accurate, eminently fair and even sympathetic expositions which he gives of the thought of his chosen exemplars. But perhaps what is most valuable in the book are the acute and sometimes devastating critical questions which he raises.

On the general question of the appropriateness of applying empiricism to the problems of religion, Martin's principal objection seems to be that in the process 'empiricism' is subtly redefined and various non-empirical factors are unobtrusively introduced. Thus, in the case of Brightman, it is claimed that he began by thinking of empiricism as being concerned with sense-experience, but then so broadened the concept of experience that Martin is compelled to write: 'When empirical method is equated with all the ways of the mind involved in inquiry, it loses any specific connotation and makes alternative methods unthinkable.'[6] The attempt by Macintosh to construct an empirical theology is criticized on the grounds that he 'really presupposes many of the insights of "normative" or "valuational" theology in what he takes to be the strictly "empirical" part of the whole enterprise'.[7] Wieman's claim to be using 'scientific method' is put in question, according to Martin, by the fact that he uses the expression 'very broadly' and that 'in its application to religious problems, it differs significantly from the working procedures of the exact sciences'.[8]

These criticisms of the uses of the methods of empiricism in philosophy of religion are damaging enough, since they point to basic confusions and ambiguities. They suggest that the wrong tools are being used for the job, and that the subject-matter of religion is not amenable to investigation by methods and concepts which have their proper home elsewhere. Incidentally, this might imply that similar objections will apply to empiricist critiques of religion, but we shall come to this later.

Martin follows up his general criticisms of the methods of the empiricist philosophers of religion with further and more specific probing of the content of some of these philosophies. For instance, he claims that the concepts of God developed by Brightman and Wieman would seem to be religiously very inadequate and certainly not able to bear the weight of meaning which Christian theology places on the word 'God'.

In the decades that have elapsed since the publication of Martin's book, I do not believe that empiricist attempts to develop a philosophy of religion have made any significant progress, so that the kind of criticisms which Martin raised still remain unanswered. Let me cite just one example, the English philosopher of religion, Ian Ramsey. Trained in the natural sciences and teaching in an atmosphere saturated with philosophical empiricism, he felt strongly attracted to the project of constructing an empiricist philosophy of religion. No one will question the apologetic value of his writings or the pioneering work that he did on the problems of religious language. But I do not think he can be rightly called a 'Christian empiricist'. The foundation stone of his philosophy of religion is what he called the 'disclosure situation'. He describes this as 'a situation where I am confronted in principle with the whole universe'.[9] This sounds almost like a revelation, and is scarcely a notion that one would expect to meet in a strictly empiricist thinker. It suggests a mystical or metaphysical vision, though I think there are reasons to believe that it was from Bultmann and so ultimately from existentialism that Ramsey adopted the language of 'disclosure'.

I have indicated that even as empiricism fails to construct an affirmative philosophy of religion, so it also fails to demolish the claims of religion, because in both cases it is on the wrong wave-length, so to speak. I shall illustrate this from a brief consideration of the book *Contemporary Critiques of Religion*, by Kai Nielsen, who for many years has been a stern critic of Christianity, theism and religious belief in general. In the book, he sets out the empiricist case against religion and theology, as it has developed (or, perhaps I should say, atrophied) from the 1930s onward. He takes as his starting point Ayer's famous onslaught on religious belief. But Nielsen is a very honest thinker. He admits that the early logical empiricists drew far more from their analysis than they were entitled to draw. Of Ayer and those who thought like him, Nielsen says that 'they have so modified their positions that they no longer hold the iconoclastic position that was so distinctive of logical empiricism'.[10] The verification principle itself has been called in question and is of doubtful status. The claim that the meaning of a statement is the method of its verification (always a very obscure dogma) is rejected by Nielsen, who makes the rather obvious point that only if one knows what a statement means could one ask about how to verify it. Since it was on this issue that the old empiricists decided that religious statements are meaningless, Nielsen reduces the charge to one of incoherence. But he has a hard job trying to make his case and he acknowledges the strength of counter-critiques, such as those of Plantinga. The whole book in fact is a series of modifications and retrenchments, in which the once-sweeping demolition of the religious case has been rolled back bit by bit until we reach the stage *quo ante bellum erat*, that is to say, the stage with which we have been familiar for a very long time when neither the defender of religion nor his opponent can deliver a finally demonstrative argument. Reading Nielsen's review of the empiricist critique over the past fifty years, one cannot help being reminded of some words of another empiricist, used in a quite different connection a generation ago: 'A fine brash hypothesis may be killed by inches, the death of a thousand qualifications.'[11]

I have already made it clear that I do not think that empiricism has simply been exploded, either as a general philosophical stance or in its application to religion. But enough weaknesses have been brought to light over the years to show that there is some deep-seated sickness here. At the very least, it is a legitimate demand that the dominance of empiricism in the philosophical world should be challenged, and other ways of philosophizing given a fair hearing.

4

Systematic Theology and Biblical Studies

At the present time, systematic theology and biblical studies have drifted apart. In some measure, this is part of the price we pay for specialization. What theologian can keep up with the work being done in systematics and philosophy of religion, and at the same time be familiar with the vast amount of work being done on the New Testament, to say nothing of the Old? Edward Schillebeeckx may be such a one, but he is a solitary figure and some have questioned the extent of his competence in New Testament scholarship. It is even rarer to find a New Testament scholar who is at home in systematic theology and religious philosophy. Perhaps Rudolf Bultmann was the last. Not only have the two disciplines diverged, there is also some suspicion between them. Systematic theologians try to make themselves independent of the changing theories of biblical scholars, while the latter complain that the work of the theologians is unsound because they have not taken into account the most recent researches into the Bible.

All this, of course, is a vast departure from the days when systematic theology was understood as an ordered presentation of biblical teaching. The last major example of this was Karl Barth's *Church Dogmatics*, but the temper of modern theology is better represented by Paul Tillich's *Systematic Theology*, in which you can read long stretches with not a mention of the Bible.

I mentioned Bultmann as a New Testament scholar who had both critical and theological interests and was also competent in some areas of philosophy (though Jaspers considered his philosophical range to be very narrow). Yet even Bultmann tended to keep his critical New Testament scholarship and his demythologized theology apart. His existential interpretation of the New Testament is in many ways a continuation of Lutheran evangelical pietism, and one could read his sermons without suspecting that he was also the author of books of radical criticism.

I do not think myself we can have theology without the Bible, or theology in which the Bible has been reduced to a very subordinate position. Perhaps I should say, we cannot have *Christian* theology. No doubt one might try to launch a new religion, with a purely rationalist theology or perhaps a syncretistic theology derived from half a dozen religious traditions. Some contemporary theologians seem to be moving in these directions and to have cut so many links with the Bible that they are near to offering us a new religion. But I wonder if they have considered the difficulties. I can't help remembering the story of the French philosopher who decided that Christianity was outmoded, and asked a bishop how he might go about founding a new religion. 'Go and be crucified, and rise again on the third day', was the reply.

But why insist on this link with the Bible, if indeed it is so distant from our time as to be scarcely intelligible, and if it is filled with the cultural presuppositions of an alien era? I suppose the answer is that it is the Bible that defines what Christianity is and what it can become. Here is the original and, indeed, the only witness we have to the birth of Christianity. Anything that claims to be Christian theology must be able to demonstrate that it stands in recognizable continuity with the documents that define what Christianity is. Of course, this does not mean that we are to fall into the opposite error of trying to get right back to the origin and to confront the figure of Jesus as he appeared to the first Jewish disciples. This would be impossible, because we can only read these texts in the light of the theological tradition in which they have been transmitted to us. Admittedly, we can try to become more aware of this preunderstanding that we bring to the texts, and we can even become critical of it. But we can never jump out of our place in history and see Jesus as if for the first time. And even if we could, what would we make of him? Furthermore, the attempt to get back to the beginnings forgets that any great event needs time for its proper appreciation. The first naive understanding of Jesus by the disciples in terms of their Jewish tradition was only a faltering first step. It had to be succeeded by further and deeper reflection. Already by the time John's Gospel came to be written, thinking about the meaning of Jesus Christ had gone a long way. This thinking continued after the New Testament period through the patristic period and the formation of the classical creeds, and it goes on to the present day.

Anthony Thiselton has recently written: 'Systematic theology might be said to represent the end process to date of that long growth of tradition in which the Christian community has struggled to arrive at an interpretation of the biblical texts which both does justice to its own present place in tradition and seeks to discard those false prejudgments which have proved unfruitful.'[1]

The quotation is taken from a book called *The Two Horizons*. A horizon is the boundary which limits the view to be seen from any particular spot. Dr Thiselton is using the word in its technical sense to mean the world-view that people have at any given time in a history and culture, all that is included in their outlook. The two horizons of his title are, on the one hand, the horizon of the New Testament writers and, on the other, the horizon of today. The work of the systematic theologian is to bring about a 'fusion' of these horizons, so that what found expression within the horizon of the first-century writers can be re-expressed within our horizon. Notice also that his remark about systematic theology recognizes that it has a twofold task, both constructive and critical. It aims at interpreting Christian truth for its own time, but also at discarding unfruitful elements that may have been thrown up in the tradition.

At this point, it is worthwhile noting a distinction between exegesis and interpretation. Exegesis is primarily the concern of biblical scholars. For this work, they need much linguistic, historical and literary expertise. Their aim is to establish, as far as this is possible, what the writer had in mind when he wrote the words. Interpretation, on the other hand, is concerned with conveying the meaning of a text to one's own contemporaries. It is a difficult operation, demanding both a faithfulness to the governing intention of the text and an honesty in regard to contemporary ways of under-standing. Although there is a science of interpretation (hermeneutics) it is widely agreed that interpretation is an art as well as a science, and that it cannot be done just by rules and techniques but needs a creative act. In part, this is because language always says more than the author was aware of when he wrote. In Gadamer's words, 'Not occasion-ally, but always, a text goes beyond its author. That is why understanding is not merely a reproductive but a productive act as well.'[2]

But does this not open the door to putting on a text any interpretation we please? Are we not embarked on the construction of a new religion just as much as those who more or less explicitly discard the Bible, except that we are being less honest and claiming that our interpretation can be derived from the text – if not from what it says, then from what it does not say?

Undoubtedly, that is a constant danger. There occurs not a fusion of horizons, but the supplanting of the New Testa-ment horizon by a modern one, and then we construct a picture that fits our modern presuppositions but may have no solid foundation in the original text. This was the kind of thing Schweitzer criticized in his study of the nineteenth-century attempts to write the life of Jesus. It is still a danger. Dr Thiselton warns us, 'We must not construct a portrait of Jesus which merely bounces back to us our own viewpoints and assumptions.'[3]

It is here, I think, that the critical and exegetical work of New Testament scholars becomes important for the work of the systematic theologian. I said already that the theologian of today cannot seek to go back to the beginnings as if nothing had happened in the intervening centuries, as if there had been no deepening and development of theology.

That would be like being content with an acorn, rather than the majestic oak that has sprung from it. But there is also a justifiable return to the sources. Not all development is legitimate. There are branches that need to be pruned, boughs that need to be lopped off. Critical study of the New Testament and precise exegesis can help to show the systematic theologian where interpretations have moved so far from the sources that they cannot legitimately claim to be derived from Christianity as set out in its source documents. For instance, the politicized picture of Jesus as a revolutionary that has been popular in some quarters in recent years is contradicted by critical study of the source. This, of course, does not mean that the gospel has no political implications, but it does rule out that particular interpretation as a mere subjective imagining.

Another way in which the systematic theologian must take account of biblical studies has to do with the plurality of theologies in the New Testament. Older theologians would appeal indiscriminately to Paul, John, Mark and the rest. The modern theologian must be much more careful.

We begin to see more clearly why the interpretative work of the theologian is both science and art. He directs his questions to the text, and these questions inevitably get shaped in terms of his own horizon and interests. Yet he must not, as it were, dominate the text with these questions. The text has got to be allowed to speak, and then interpretation becomes reciprocal. The text reacts on the questions we put, and suggests new and other questions. It is in this situation that one can rightly speak of an art, for it is a question of balancing one thing against another, of maintaining right proportions.

It is here too that one may introduce the word 'meditation'. The work of the theologian includes deep meditation on the meaning of the text, and this is not so much a conscious seeking or an active investigation as simply a remaining open to the possibility of receiving an insight into the apparently inexhaustible fund of meaning which lies hid in the New Testament. Obviously, such meditation is not far removed from some forms of prayer.

There are other sources of theology besides the Bible, most notably the tradition of the church, representing its collective experience and wisdom, and, in addition, one's own experience, for however fragmentary it may be, we could hardly have a vital belief in anything unless it were somehow confirmed in our experience. Yet among these sources the Bible has pre-eminent place, and certainly this is true in the Anglican tradition. We must remember, however, that the sources I have mentioned are all subordinate to Jesus Christ himself, the living Word. The Bible is not the ultimate source, though it is the indispensable testimony to that source. It is right, therefore, that these documents be scrutinized and analysed as far as can be done, so that they may speak to us as truly as is possible. The theologian then must welcome the work of biblical scholars and pay attention to it in his own work. Yet he will believe – and I hope without any arrogance – that the work of technical biblical scholarship is a preliminary to the all-important task of trying to hear and pass on God's word for our day.

5

Tradition, Truth and Christology

Both 'tradition' and 'truth' are difficult and complex concepts. More than that, their meanings have varied from one context to another. The notion of 'tradition' not only refers to a continuous history of ideas and practices but has itself a history in the course of which it has been understood in different ways. On the other hand, the notion of 'truth' is an obvious example of a polymorphous concept. Not only do the words 'true' and 'truth' bear a wide variety of meanings in the ordinary language which reflects common sense; the same holds also at the more sophisticated level of different sciences and intellectual disciplines. Our task, then, is to attempt to clarify these concepts and to show their bearing in particular upon the problem of christology.

Let us begin by considering tradition. Perhaps the first point to notice is the obvious and rather sharp contrast between what may be called 'static' and 'dynamic' ways of understanding tradition. On the static view, tradition was understood as a body of propositional material, a deposit of truth, existing alongside scripture and supplementing it. The relation of tradition to scripture was indeed a complicated matter. Clearly, there must have been an oral tradition that antedated scripture. Then again, some of this traditional material may have survived alongside scripture without being incorporated into it. It must, moreover, have been on the basis of traditions of authorship and authenticity that the canon of scripture was fixed. And finally, tradition came to include creeds and dogmatic definitions which did indeed claim to be based on scripture, but which then acquired a measure of independence as norms for the interpretation of scripture. This body of traditional material, it was supposed, had been carefully preserved and transmitted unchanged from generation to generation.

It was this static understanding of tradition and perhaps especially the idea of a body of propositional truths supplemental to the scriptures that made the whole question of tradition so controversial in the eyes of Protestants, though one would have to add that the position was much exacerbated by their own insistence on the principle *sola scriptura*, as if scripture itself had not arisen and continued within the context of a tradition. But the static understanding of tradition has been to a large extent overcome, and been superseded by a dynamic concept which goes far to resolving some of the old conflicts between Catholics and Protestants. Vatican II's constitution on 'Divine Revelation' did not speak of two parallel deposits of truth, fixed in propositional form, but brought tradition and scripture together under the very dynamic metaphor of a single river that is flowing along: 'Hence,' it was stated, 'there exist a close connection and communication between sacred tradition and sacred scripture. For both of them, flowing from the same divine well-spring, in a certain way merge into a unity and tend toward the same end.'[1] A contributor to *Sacramentum Mundi* has explained the change as follows: 'One of the great achievements of Vatican II was to free the Catholic notion of tradition from the narrow limits to which it had been confined, chiefly in the post-Tridentine period. In the dogmatic constitution on revelation, tradition does not appear primarily as a certain amount of matter, always the same, handed on in propositions and practices. The tradition of the church is rather faith as lived.' The writer then quotes a sentence from Vatican II: 'The church, in her teaching, life and worship, perpetuates and hands on to all generations all that she herself is, all that she believes.'[2]

It is interesting to note that this writer holds that the static, propositional view of tradition has prevailed 'chiefly in the post-Tridentine period'. One can find evidences of a more dynamic conception in earlier times. Vincent of Lerins' famous formula, 'that which has been believed everywhere, always and by all', is often quoted by those who think in terms of an unchanging deposit, but what one hears much less frequently quoted are some other words of Vincent from this same writing of his, where he says that 'there should be a great increase and vigorous progress in the individual man as well as in the entire church as the ages and the centuries march on, of understanding, knowledge and wisdom'.[3] This surely expresses a dynamic understanding of tradition, comparable to the image of the flowing stream which we have noted in Vatican II. Incidentally, although Vatican II makes no reference to Vincent of Lerins, there is such close verbal agreement between those words of his which I have just quoted and a passage in the constitution on 'Divine Revelation' that it can hardly have been an accident, and Vincent's words must have been in the minds of the authors of the constitution when they wrote: 'There is a growth in the understanding of the realities and of the words that have been handed down, for, as the centuries succeed one another, the church constantly moves forward toward the fullness of divine truth until the words of God reach their complete fulfilment in her.'[4]

Of course, as soon as one begins to talk in this way and to admit the occurrence of growth and deepening in understanding in the process of tradition, the question about the nature of this growth must arise. Is it simply the explicitation, the unfolding, of what was given in the beginning? Or must it not be the case that as the given comes to be better understood and as it is brought into contact with new conceptions and new historical situations and new developments of knowledge, it will itself have new dimensions which it would be hard to claim were already there in the beginning? And if one admits the possibility of the emergence of the new within the transmission of tradition, then is one not also admitting the possibility of change, and would not such change be an undermining of the very nature of tradition?

It is not easy to answer these questions, but we must not think that there is a simple disjunction between the view that the development of tradition is purely explicitation of what was there in the beginning and the view that such development brings novelties that must be accounted as departures from the beginning. On the one hand, there may well have been possibilities or potentialities hidden in the beginning, and such that new concepts and new circumstances could bring them to light. On the other hand, the concept of change implies continuity just as much as difference. Bernard Lonergan has offered this useful definition of change: 'If there is change, there has to be a concrete unity of concrete data extending over some interval of time, there has to be some difference between the data at the beginning and at the end of the interval, and this difference can be only partial, for otherwise there would occur not a change but an annihilation and a new creation.'[5] A dynamic understanding of tradition can, I think, allow for development that can properly be called change, but clearly the identity that underlies the change must remain recognizable. Some innovations might be so drastic that they could not be counted as developments of the Christian tradition but as its replacement with a new religion. Such innovations might be sudden, or they might come about by a long series of minute changes, each hardly noticed, until the point was reached when the tradition had been virtually abandoned. Some people have in fact claimed that since its beginnings Christianity has undergone so much change that the faith that Christians hold today is quite different from and discontinuous with the faith of the first believers. I think that it cannot be denied that it is very different, but I also think that it is an exaggeration to deny some persistent elements of continuity. However, this raises a difficult question to which we must return later – the question of what developments of the tradition are legitimate and what criteria we might have for testing their legitimacy.

In the meanwhile, let us look more closely at the structure of tradition, and this will enable us to grasp more clearly what is meant by a dynamic tradition. In any tradition, it is possible to distinguish three constitutive elements: first, the origin, the truth or insight from which the tradition took its rise and which it is intended to perpetuate; second, the transmission, the actual process of passing on, and we have seen that this may include deepening and development; third, there is the reception and appropriation of the truth by those living at any particular point of time to which the tradition had reached. The question about the initial truth is one that can be left until we come to our more extended discussion of truth. We turn immediately then to the question of transmission.

In the Christian church, there are quite specific vehicles for the transmission of the tradition. Preaching is the most fundamental, and has gone on continuously since the time of the apostles. Alongside preaching, we may set the work of teaching, especially the instruction of catechumens. The earliest preaching and teaching, *kerygma* and *didache*, antedated the writing of the Gospels – indeed, according to the form critics, the Synoptic Gospels were constructed out of units of such preaching and teaching. Today, the preacher will base himself most likely on some passage of scripture, but his handling of it will be shaped by a great deal of tradition that he has received – the teaching to which he himself was exposed in his training, the credal and doctrinal material of his church, classic expositions of the text by fathers of the church, ancient or modern, the works of commentators, widely received interpretations and so on. Another major vehicle for transmission is constituted by the sacraments. In them, the members of the Christian community relive the creative moments from which their tradition has sprung. The believer is buried with Christ in baptism and raised with him to newness of life. The participant in the eucharistic liturgy recalls the sacrificial death of Christ and is brought into communion with him. What we are talking about here is not the mere preservation and passing on of carefully conserved propositions or fossilized practices, but very much a living tradition. That presupposes in turn a continuing community, and that is why the notion of apostolic succession includes not only the abstract idea of a succession in apostolic truth but its concrete counterpart, a living succession of apostolic teachers.

The reception and appropriation of the tradition by those

living at any particular time occurs when, through their exposure to preaching and teaching and through their participation in the sacramental life of the Christian community, that original truth or insight from which the tradition came makes its impact upon them too and is received by them. To be sure, it will not be identical in every successive period, but if we are to speak of a continuing tradition or even of a continuing Christian religion, rather than the invention of new religions, there must be a discernible measure of identity between what is received today and what stood at the beginning of the tradition as its origin.

Here a difficult and somewhat speculative question arises. Is it the tradition, or only the tradition, that makes available to us the original truth? Is it not rather that the origin can still be present with us, and this is what we mean when we speak of the risen Christ or of the Holy Spirit? When, for instance, the word of preaching is heard and received, is not this the risen Christ speaking to his people through the words of the sermon, or the Holy Spirit bringing to life the words of scripture so that we understand them as words directed to us in our situation? Or again, is not the living Christ present himself in the eucharist, so that the recalling of him is no mere subjective remembrance of his past reality now transmitted by the traditional words and gestures, but a present participation in his life? I certainly would not wish to deny any of these points, but the full discussion of them would take us into areas of theology extending far beyond the topics of this lecture. But I would point out that even if we say that Christ or the Holy Spirit is at work today among the faithful, nevertheless such action normally takes place through the vehicles of tradition that form part of the church's life. I cannot, of course, exclude the possibility that in exceptional cases individuals may have the experience of a direct mystical communion with Christ, or may receive a private interior illumination of the Spirit. But Christianity is a communal rather than a private religion, and for the vast majority of its adherents, any experience they may have of God's word or God's presence comes on occasions of preaching, teaching, sacramental action and any other way

in which that which has been received from the past is
handed on and renewed in the present. If indeed the risen
Christ or the Holy Spirit is active in this, that fact does not
render preaching, sacraments and the rest unimportant or
make the process of transmission superfluous. The notions
of divine presence and human transmission are not opposed
but complementary. As D. Wiederkehr has recently
remarked: 'It would be over-enthusiastic to imagine that the
ecclesiological making-present in human historical activity,
tradition, witness and proclamation, are made superfluous
by the pneumatological category of mediation. The New
Testament sees the witness of the Spirit and the human
witness of the Church not as competitors but as two currents
that conjoin, each making the other possible. ''But when the
Counsellor comes, whom I shall send to you from the Father,
even the Spirit of truth . . . he will bear witness to me; and
you also are witnesses, because you have been with me from
the beginning'' (John 15. 26–27).'[6]

Now that we have raised the question of the relation of
Christ to the Christian tradition, this may be the appropriate
moment to take up the deferred question of the origin of the
tradition. What is that wellspring from which the tradition
has flowed? This is also to raise the question about truth,
for we are asking about the nature of the truth which the
tradition is supposed to pass on.

I think we must say that just as we have rejected the static
view of tradition, according to which it was conceived as a
body of fixed propositions, so we must also reject a static
propositional conception of truth, at least in the context of
theology. Many theologians, both Protestant and Catholic,
have in recent decades turned away from a propositional
view of revelation. They do not abandon the concept of
revelation or its accompanying claim to truth, but they hold
that prior to any propositional formulations of faith is the
person and work of Jesus Christ, his life, death and resurrec-
tion. It is this person who is himself the revelation and the
origin of the tradition. Yet, to speak more accurately, it is
not simply Jesus Christ in himself but what theologians call
the 'Christ-event' that originates the tradition. By the 'Christ-

event' is meant both the revelation and its reception, for indeed one could scarcely speak of a revelation unless it were received. I would be in agreement with Paul Tillich when he writes, 'Christianity was born, not with the birth of the man who is called Jesus, but in the moment in which one of his followers was driven to say of him, "You are the Christ!" '[7] In the sense that revelation includes in itself reception, that means that the revelation, the original insight at the beginning of the tradition, is itself a handing over, but here the one who hands over is God himself. It was Karl Barth who pointed out that the same Greek verb, *paradidonai*, is used both for the human handing over of tradition and for God's handing over of his Son, which is not only the origin of the tradition but the original tradition or handing over.[8] This was the revelation and reception, the moment of truth that constituted the origin of the Christian faith and that the tradition, with its apparatus of preaching, sacraments and so on, seeks to perpetuate and hand over again and again.

But what understanding of truth is implied here? It cannot be a static truth to be enshrined in propositional formulae which can then lie around in text-books to be available for reference when required. The truth we are talking about here is event, the event of revelation and reception, the event of the Father's handing over the Son which is also the event of the divine self-communication, the event which is the paradigm for all subsequent handing over, *paradosis*, tradition.

Truth, in Christian theology, is event, and specifically the Christ-event. There is an early indication of this in John's Gospel, where the Lord says of himself, 'I am the truth' (John 14.6). To say of a person that he is the truth is, of course, a most uncommon usage, but it is a good illustration of the way in which language itself develops to express new realities and in which words acquire new dimensions of meaning. Truth is here being given a dynamic sense. The Christ-event, it is claimed, is the truth-event, the event which brings into the light the realities of the human condition and the reality of God.

There is an influential school of modern philosophy which has greatly clarified this way of understanding truth. One may mention first of all Kierkegaard's distinction between objective truths, truths of empirical fact expressed in propositions that can be written down or printed in books and instantly appropriated by anyone who cares to read them; and what he misleadingly called subjective truths, the kind that have to be inwardly appropriated, sometimes with much pain, and which cannot be instantly seized because they are inseparable from the way that leads to them. This is truth as event, truth as the attainment of insight into the basic human condition. Heidegger's reflections on truth are similar, though differently expressed. He begins from the etymology of the Greek word for truth, *aletheia*, literally 'unhiddenness' or 'unconcealedness'. The event of truth takes place when concealments and distortions are removed, and something is exposed as it really is. In Heidegger, too, there is stress on appropriation as an essential part of the truth-event. Man's special status in the universe is seen as his openness, so that he is like a clearing amid the opacity of things and thus has the possibility of receiving and standing in the truth, or, it may be, of missing it. Finally, one may mention Gadamer's remarkable treatment of the truth of an art work, which has obvious implications for theology. According to Gadamer, art is no less concerned with truth than is science, though these are different ways to truth. The work of art reveals or uncovers the very essence of that which it represents, so that Gadamer can even claim that we see that essence more clearly in the work of art than in the original itself. This essence is at first grasped by the artist, but through the art work which he creates the same insight into truth is provided for those to whom that work communicates.

Let me pause at this point to sum up the way by which we have come so far. We have been determined to break out of older, static ways of understanding both tradition and truth, and have tried to understand both of these in a dynamic way. Thus we found the origin of the tradition in the living truth of Christ himself, indeed in that archetypal *paradosis* or *traditio* which is the event of God's self-communication in Christ. Such an event certainly includes language – for instance, Christ's teaching – as all human realities do, but it is something broader and deeper than language and cannot be wholly reduced to a set of propositions. This implies also that for its transmission and perpetuation it needs more than verbal formulae, more even than preaching and teaching, for it needs a living community. In such a community the Christ-event is, so to speak, constantly re-enacted, the revelation and its reception continue to take place. Thus it is the living community itself that is the vehicle for the transmission of the tradition, though we have noted that within the community there are specialized vehicles or organs such as preaching and the sacraments for recalling and re-presenting the creative truth. Finally, when this is received today, the faithful still participate in the original vision. But we did also note that our experience today will not be identical with that of the first disciples, and could not be so. Traditions are inevitably subject to development, change and even decay. A tradition may wander so far from its original meaning that it becomes something quite different, though if that happens, it surely ceases to be the tradition that it claims to be. How then can a tradition and its development be kept sound? How do we criticize and assess tradition? How among the developments it brings forth do we know what to receive and what to reject?

Perhaps the first answer to this question must be a pragmatic one. If the function of tradition is to perpetuate and renew the original moment of truth, then whatever in the tradition does speak to us and illuminates our own lives in a convincing way is in fact doing the work for which it is intended, and is to be gladly received. But if there is something else in the tradition that causes us puzzlement and may stand in the way of our participating in Christian truth, then even if it may have spoken to people in the past, it must now be called into question. This may not mean that it is simply to be discarded, but it may demand a radical rethinking. But while it is easy to state this broad pragmatic principle of discrimination, it is much more difficult to apply it, and this is the point where it needs to be refined and developed into a hermeneutic of tradition. But then one soon strikes sharp differences of opinion. Let me illustrate briefly from the question of christology.

At one extreme, we find the attempt to get back to the purity of the origin, to the unvarnished truth of Jesus before the long process of tradition had got to work. The most famous representative of this point of view was Adolf Harnack, who tried to strip away the successive layers of theological interpretation and speculation laid down by the developing tradition so as to get back to the originating event in its pristine state. The development of christological dogma, he believed, was a decline from the far more impressive reality of the human historical Jesus. This point of view is still represented today, notably by Don Cupitt, who declares that: 'Christianity quickly evolved so far away from the outlook and values of Jesus that it has been scarcely justified in using his name at all.'[9]

Clearly, those who think in this way have a somewhat negative evaluation of tradition. They prize the origin, and believe that the tradition that springs from it is more likely to be a falling away than a deepening and development. In particular, they think of christological dogma as obscuring the reality of Christ, and their aim is not the negative one of dismantling dogma but the affirmative one of setting free the original revelation.

One has also to say that there are many considerations that favour this approach. Whatever may be true in the case of the natural sciences, it would seem that in art, philosophy and religion, the great moment of illumination comes at the beginning, and that what follows is often a levelling down and a deterioration. We might well agree with Heidegger that 'the beginning is the strangest and the mightiest'.[10] But even if one allows this weight to the origin – and anyone who accepts that Christianity rests on a divine revelation would seem bound to allow it – nevertheless, one is also bound to allow time for its appropriation and comprehension, for revelation, as we have seen, must include its reception. The significance of the Christ-event was not grasped in that first moment when Peter confessed, 'You are the Christ!' That was only a first approximation that needed a lot of teasing out and interpretation. The significance was not grasped in its fullness by the time the last book of the New Testament was written, though certainly there had been many new developments. The process was not completed at Chalcedon, nor is it complete at the present day, if within the living tradition of the Christ-event the encounter of Christ with the faithful is still taking place. Let us agree that in the course of nineteen centuries the tradition has thrown up many false and misleading developments. That is why we need to keep going back to the origins to ensure that the tradition remains true to them. But the fact that mistakes have been made cannot justify the belief that the tradition as a whole is misleading, or the attempt to leap back over the centuries to a supposed original uncontaminated understanding of Christ.

On the contrary, one has to face the question raised by Gadamer whether a certain amount of distancing is not necessary before any event can be properly understood and evaluated. Just as we need to stand back from a work of art if we are to see it properly, so, it is argued, we must be at a certain distance in time before an historical event reveals its contours and significance. I have suggested that the understanding of the Christ-event took quite some time and may still be going on. However, one could also raise the question whether there is an optimum distance or range of distance, for obviously the event begins to fade when the distance becomes too great. In his *Critique of Judgment*, Kant instances the case of the Pyramids, the effect of which can be appreciated only if one avoids either coming too near or staying too far away.[11] If there is such an optimum range of distance in the case of the Christ-event, then this would be the period for the formation of what might be called the 'classic' or 'catholic' tradition concerning the event, and this classic tradition would have more weight and would have discerned more than the immediate original perception of the event, assuming that we could recapture it. This classic statement of the tradition would, along with the return to origins, begin to function as a norm for judging subsequent developments in the tradition.

At the opposite extreme from those who want to leap over tradition to the beginning, we find those who want to discard the beginning. The original Christ-event, they tell us, is too distant in time for us to know much about it, and in any case it took place in a culture so alien to our own as to be inaccessible to our understanding. What we know for a fact is that there exists today a Christian community where men and women experience forgiveness, reconciliation and a new relation both with God and with one another. It is with this present community and what it provides that we must be concerned, not with its origins. 'Discovering the Christian gospel for today is a task for the Christians of today.'[12] That sentence is a quotation from Dennis Nineham, to whom, I think, the view that I have outlined could be not unfairly attributed.

Here again we find a very negative attitude to tradition, and again we can acknowledge that there are some points in its favour. The Christian church has often been preoccupied with its own past and has become the victim of a harmful traditionalism which has prevented engagement with the questions of discipleship in the modern age. Yet when that is conceded, there is surely an unacceptable arbitrariness in the claim that is made for a community that has come out of an unknown past and leads into an unknown future. Perhaps such a view reflects something of the rootlessness or what sociologists call the 'anomie' of our twentieth-century Western culture. But it is also an extraordinarily triumphalist view of the church, which would have to stand on its own claim to be the people of God, without pointing to any originating act of God. Can the church, the church as we see it today, have any claim on our allegiance unless that is part of the superior claim of Jesus Christ? Is not the very existence of this community evidence of the decisive significance of its origin? Nineham's view of the church is close to that of the American John Knox, but differs sharply in an important respect, for Knox holds that Jesus Christ himself and the experience of the primitive church 'have a normative significance which the experience and thought of the church in no later period can have'.[13] This, I would have thought, can alone give the present-day church credibility.

We have briefly considered and criticized two extreme contemporary reactions to the place of tradition when we seek the truth about Christ. Between them lies a more dialectical approach which does not lead to such clean-cut results but calls for that patient wrestling with the significance of Jesus Christ which has in fact characterized the mainstream of the church's thinking through the ages. It rejects all one-sided solutions. It acknowledges both the normative status of the origins and the legitimacy of that mainstream of development which has come from the wellspring and has been acknowledged by the consensus of the Christian community. It acknowledges the time-conditioned character of even the most authoritative verbal formulations, but tries sympathetically to understand the governing intention behind them and to re-express whatever is true in it. The pronouncements of the tradition are neither to be thoughtlessly accepted nor thoughtlessly rejected, but pondered, deepened, sifted and rethought. No doubt this is a difficult task, and one that will have no end as long as the church remains, but it is the way toward ensuring a living tradition that will be the vehicle of a living truth and that will extend the blessings of the Christ-event to future generations.

6

The Anthropological
Approach to Theology

Christian theology is concerned with a single comprehensive truth – the truth of God in Jesus Christ. If we possessed the intellectual powers which Denys attributed to the higher celestial beings, we would be able to grasp that truth intuitively in all its fullness. We would receive its total illumination, without obscurities and without distortions. Incidentally, such a state of affairs would render at a stroke all theologians redundant, and their painstaking work, from the careful study of texts to the frustrating search for words in which to give a contemporary interpretation, would be unnecessary. So perhaps it is just as well that we are mere human beings, that our thought proceeds discursively from point to point, that our theology is broken down into manageable units – dogmas, propositions, arguments, opinions. It follows inevitably that any theology will have its blind spots as well as its illuminations and that it will get some things out of proportion. If these defects are to be avoided (so far as it is possible) then the theologian must constantly bear in mind the underlying unity of the truth he seeks, and make explicit the organic connection that links all the items which enter into his theological statement. This means in turn that there must be some unifying perspective, not imposed from outside but drawn from within the matter of theology itself.

Another consequence that follows from what has already been said is that within Christian theology it ought to be possible to take any single doctrine as a starting point, and from it to work through the whole corpus of truth. For if the whole has the organic character that I have claimed for it, then each item belonging to it must, like a Leibnizian monad, be a mirror of the whole. I do believe that any Christian doctrine could serve as a point from which one could reach out into the whole texture of theology, but I do not want to suggest that it is a matter of indifference where one begins. Clearly, the beginning establishes a perspective, and gives a certain character to the complete theological enterprise. Some doctrines are more central and have more ramifications than others. Such a doctrine would be more likely to lead us into an inclusive and balanced appreciation of the whole than a doctrine that is more peripheral and not so obviously interwoven with the others. Again, there is always the danger that theology may turn into an abstruse intellectual exercise, so it is important to select a doctrine that has existential as well as logical connections with other doctrines and that will therefore keep before us soteriological concerns, so reminding us that Christian theology has spiritual as well as scientific interests.

Here I want to state the claims for anthropology or the doctrine of man as an area of study which fulfils many of the requirements I have just outlined. I make these claims not only because I have myself been long convinced of their validity, but because the distinguished theologian in whose honour this lecture is being given, Dr Rahner, has employed the anthropological approach in an extraordinarily fruitful way and the estimate we make of his contribution to theology must in large measure depend upon our opinion about the validity of this way into theological problems.

For obviously the matter is a controversial one. Many of the greatest theologians of the past have begun their investigations not from the human end but directly with God, and since theology is precisely discourse about God, it might seem that they were correct in this, and that to begin with anthropology can lead only to a humanism, tricked out perhaps with some Christian terminology but never really finding its way into a genuine theology. So we find St Thomas in his great work beginning with God, his existence, our knowledge of him, his knowledge, will and providence, his triunity and so on, before he turns to the created order, including the human race. The most systematic theologian of the Reformation, John Calvin, begins his exposition of Christian theology by acknowledging the close connection between the knowledge of God and the knowledge of ourselves. 'Our wisdom,' he claims, 'in so far as it ought to be deemed true and solid wisdom, consists almost entirely of two parts: the knowledge of God and of ourselves. But as these are connected together by many ties, it is not easy to determine which of the two precedes and gives birth to the other.'[1] But he goes on to say that a correct method requires us to begin with the knowledge of God, and only in the light of that can we hope to attain to a true self-knowledge. To these two classic exponents of Christianity we may add the greatest Protestant theologian of the present century, Karl Barth. His *Church Dogmatics* begins with the Word of God and he is uncompromising in denying that there is any way by which the human mind could rise from its finite and sinful condition to any genuine theological insight. Natural theology is dismissed as a sinful and arrogant attempt to turn God into an object at our disposal; religion is described as man's attempt to grasp God, and contrasted with the Christian revelation which moves in the opposite direction; there is declared to be no analogy of being (*analogia entis*) relating humanity and deity, and Barth does not conceal his belief that the doctrine of an *analogia entis* is little short of blasphemous. So the weight of opinion among the great theologians would not seem to favour the anthropological approach.

Yet even if the classical approach – and I suppose Barth can be regarded as a late flowering of classical theology, indeed, a conscious imitator of the Reformers – considered it right to place the doctrine of God at the forefront of theology, it does not follow that this approach remains valid for all time or that circumstances might not arise in which it had become simply inappropriate. I believe that in fact such circumstances have now overtaken us. For the first time in history, we find ourselves living in the age of the godless man. I do not mean that we are living in the midst of explicit atheism, though indeed there is a good deal of openly professed atheism, and it is even the officially supported creed of several large and powerful countries. I refer rather to implicit atheism, to the fact that the very concept of God has faded in large measure from the modern consciousness. There was a time when 'God' was a word of everyday use. God's commands were thought to determine what is right and what is wrong; God's providence was supposed to govern the course of this world's happenings, which might then be interpreted as evidences of divine favour or disapproval; in the face of suffering or privation, prayer to God was the natural response. But that whole manner of God-talk has virtually disappeared, together with the beliefs which underlay it. Not only physics and chemistry and astronomy, but ethics and history and human behaviour are discussed and investigated and even (by some rash spirits) 'explained' without reference to God. The word 'God' seems to have become superfluous. Even those who profess to believe in God find it difficult to say precisely what they mean. If there really is a God, we do not find him where people once thought they found him. For a long time, he has been retreating into hiddenness, and we are uncertain where to look. We seem able to get through the day very well without any thought of God. This is what I mean by saying that we live in a godless time. There need not be the conscious or deliberate denial of God. But it cannot be denied that for a great many people he has ceased to be a reality. Dr Rahner has familiarized us with the idea of the 'anonymous Christian', the person who may intellectually profess disbelief but who existentially is committed to those values which for the Christian are concretized in God. Perhaps we should also allow for the idea of the 'anonymous atheist', the person who does not deny God and who may even persist in the outward observances of religion, but for whom it has gone dead, so to speak, and God has become an indistinct blur, the total disappearance of which would make little difference.

If theology aims, as I think it should, at expounding Christ-

ian faith in as clear and intelligible a way as the subject
matter will allow, then it must take account of the mentality
of those to whom it is addressed. The theme of theology is
and must remain God (for a theology in which 'God is dead'
is a mere contradiction), but in a godless time such as I
have described, one cannot put the doctrine of God at the
beginning. The approach must be more indirect, or the result
will be failure to communicate, misapprehension and incom-
prehension. Nor could one say that perhaps in apologetic
theology a different approach is permissible, but that in
dogmatic theology the traditional order that begins from God
must be maintained. I would reply that the distinction
between apologetics and dogmatics has now disappeared.
The mood of godlessness (which is perhaps not culpable)
has moved within the church, so that God is a problem to
the believer as well as to the unbeliever. All dogmatic
theology must therefore be at the same time an apologetic
theology, though conversely the best apologetic theology is
also dogmatic theology, letting the great Christian doctrines
be clearly seen in their own light.

It was at the time when the Enlightenment was eroding
the idea of a supernatural revelation and was even placing in
question the God of natural religion that the anthropological
approach to theology found its first powerful expression.
This, of course, was in the work of Schleiermacher. Dogmas
were declared to be, in the first instance, transcripts of
human experience, having only an indirect reference to God.
The new direction of theology, though apparent in all Schleiermacher's teaching, is especially clear in his treatment of
christology. The traditional language of descent is virtually
eliminated or radically reinterpreted, the Chalcedonian
doctrine of two natures is acutely criticized, and the heart
of the new christology is the affirmation that Christ is the
completion of the creation of humanity.[2] It was not, of
course, Schleiermacher's intention to make Christianity a
purely subjective affair, but the danger that his anthropo-
centrism could lead to such results was heavily underscored
two or three decades later when Feuerbach argued that God
is nothing but a projection of the human consciousness, an

idealized human nature which has been objectified and to which has been ascribed an independent existence. Surprisingly, Feuerbach's view has been taken up by Barth, who argues that any attempt to move from the side of the human to the divine can never arrive at any genuine knowledge of God but can end up only by putting in God's place the idolatrous projections of the human mind. But this is a dangerous game to play, for why should Barth's own thought of God be an exception? He indeed claims that it is based on a revelation coming to us from beyond ourselves and therefore possessing objectivity, but the projectionist would reply that this supposedly revealed God is, just as much as any other, a fabrication of the human mind, and his alleged objectivity is an illusion. The threat to Christian theology arising from Feuerbach and other advocates of a projection theory of religion is not confined to theologians who have employed an anthropological approach, though admittedly Feuerbach did think that Schleiermacher's teaching was a virtual admission that God has no existence beyond the subjectivity of the believer.

Barth, following Calvin, has another reason for believing that any move from the manward side towards God can lead only to an idol or false God. This is his understanding of sin. Even allowing that an understanding of the being and nature of God might be discernible in the created order, including the human being or even especially in the human being, it would be impossible for us to perceive this because our understanding is blinded and distorted by sin. Sin has infected not only the moral being of man, but his whole being, including his powers of understanding. The image of God in man has been totally defaced. To think that there is any way by which the mind can rise to the reality of God is not to take sin seriously. But what would this mean – 'not to take sin seriously'? No doubt sin has been taken with varying degrees of seriousness at different epochs of history. At the time of the Reformation, sin weighed very heavily on people's consciences. In the nineteenth century, a time of optimism and supposedly of progress, the category of sin virtually disappeared from the writings of liberal theologians. Barth and Niebuhr and others did an undoubted service in bringing back the doctrine of sin in the early decades of this century. But as the century nears its close, the earlier emphasis on sin has been muted among theologians (perhaps especially Catholic theologians) and one hears instead talk of hope and human transcendence. I come back to the question, 'What does it mean to take sin seriously?' Anyone who denies the presence of sin in human life is simply unrealistic, but it does not follow that the alternative is to ascribe to sin that totally disabling character which we find in the tradition which runs from Calvin to Barth. The scepticism which it engenders is, like all scepticism, finally self-destroying, for if the human mind is so disabled that it cannot discern any traces of God in the created order, how could it possibly recognize the presence of God in Jesus Christ? The revelation is made impossible, and so is the very idea of incarnation as God's self-communication.

Incidentally, in replying to these objections to the anthropological approach in theology, I have at the same time denied that there is any sharp distinction between natural and revealed theology, just as I earlier called in question the distinction between apologetics and dogmatics. It is not possible to reject natural theology and cling to revealed theology alone. The two stand or fall together. All natural theology is revealed theology, in the sense that, as Newman claimed, there is no 'unaided' knowledge of God, though there is a genuine self-communication of God given in and through the created order, and this may properly be called 'revelation', though it is distinct from the specific revelations of Christian and biblical faith. On the other hand, all revealed theology is natural theology, in the sense that the specific revelations of faith are communicated through this-worldly realities. To say otherwise would, I have suggested, amount to an implicit denial of the possibility of incarnation and would drive one in the direction of some docetic or gnostic view.

But now that I have at least in a provisional way, defended the anthropological approach against some of the more obvious criticisms, what is to be said affirmatively in its favour? It is to stating the affirmative case that we must now turn.

I think the first point to be made is that to begin the exposition of Christian truth from the consideration of human nature is, in a secular time, a sound educational method. If it is true that the very word 'God' has to a large extent fallen out of serious use and that even nominal believers have only the vaguest idea of what they mean by it and, for practical purposes, live as if there were no God, so that, as I suggested, not, I hope, too unkindly, they are in fact 'anonymous atheists' – if all that is so, then it would seem very odd indeed to begin expounding Christianity, even within the church, by talking about the word of God or the revelation of God. These concepts will and, in any genuinely Christian theology, must be encountered, but only further down the road. Bernard Lonergan has declared that a presupposition for entering into the study of theology is what he called 'orientation to transcendental mystery'.[3] These words were well chosen. He did not insist on an explicit belief in God, but only on openness toward transcendence. There has to be orientation and preparation before the mind that has been shaped in a godless age is able to hear in any meaningful way that word 'God', which can be both the fullest and the emptiest of all. As Martin Buber once said, the word 'God' has become the most misused and heavily burdened of all.[4] To rehabilitate this word and to let it be understood in something like its Christian sense, we have to go back to those situations where the everyday talking of the secular world has come to the end of its resources and is confronted with a mystery, the mystery which we name as 'God', though without supposing that by naming it we have also comprehended it. But to explore these situations where faith and theology have their origins is to explore the human condition. This is a low-key approach to theology, but it begins where people really are and by using the language that is current among them. And this is not just an educational or apologetic device, but can be seen as theological obedience to the incarnation, in which God came into the human condition and stood beside human beings in solidarity with them, even in their godlessness and sin. The way into theology which I have been describing may be compared with an important principle recognized by Newman and his collaborators in the Oxford Movement. This was called the 'principle of reserve'. Perhaps it reflects the divine incognito of the incarnation itself. The expression of revelation is indirect, and there is always more to be learned. The theologian who employs reserve tries not to be too explicit or exhaustive in his treatment of Christian doctrine, but holds something back in order that, having so to speak whetted the appetite of the learner, he may lead him into deeper truth and ultimately to the point where he recognizes that the deepest truth is ineffable. Only in some such way can the teacher be true to God and make sure that he does not profane the mystery. We find Newman himself writing: 'Religious men are very reserved, if only that they dare not betray, if we may so speak, God's confidence.'[5] A commentator has offered the following definition: 'Reserve is concerned with fostering the reverence due to sacred things by withholding them until men are ready to receive them.'[6] This is surely needed above all when one speaks of the final mystery of Holy Being which we name 'God'.

The connection of the foregoing remarks with the question of the appropriateness of taking anthropology as the vestibule to theology is, I think, obvious. Human nature is unquestionably a this-worldly phenomenon, and the question about the true nature and destiny of man has become for the contemporary secular person just as urgent and irresistible as the question of God appears to have become otiose and dispensable. But this question about the human being, while it begins within the horizons of the empirical, does not remain there. The empirical investigation of the human being comes up against limits where, to use the expression popularized by the sociologist Peter Berger, we receive 'signals of transcendence'.[7] Human freedom, which, in practice, is assumed by everyone, is perhaps the fundamental human characteristic that breaks out beyond the empirical. Even so severe a critic of speculative metaphysics as Kant was prepared to admit that with the knowledge of my own freedom 'the fact that a being (I myself) belonging to the world of sense, belongs also to the supersensible world, this is also positively *known*, and thus the reality of the supersensible world is established, and in practical respects *definitely* given',[8] There is hardly a modern philosophical anthropology that has not taken up the theme of human transcendence, so that if the transcendence of God has now become veiled to us, there has been a rediscovery of transcendence at the centre of human existence. This notion of transcendence plays a key role in the new expression of Thomism developed by Lonergan and others. Even neo-Marxists now speak of transcendence, and although I do not think that the actual word was used by Marx himself, something very close to the idea of transcendence was present in his philosophy. Atheistic existentialists also – Sartre is an example – have found it necessary to introduce the idea of transcendence into their analyses of human existence. All of these philosophical anthropologies have come to regard the human person as an unfinished and dynamic being, thrusting toward a fulfilment, both individual and social, that lies indefinitely ahead.

But has this human transcendence anything to do with what theologians have called the transcendence of God, or is this relocation of transcendence in the human being just one more evidence of the secularization of thought and the final erosion through the absorption of its most distinctive characteristic into the human? To this question, one may reply that the philosophers concerned have set no bounds to human transcendence. What is taking place here is not the finitization of transcendence, but the recognition of an openness in man reaching toward the infinite. Man is the finite being who nevertheless has the sense and taste for the infinite. What is the mystery constituting the goal of human transcendence if it is not God? Is not this transcendence which we find within ourselves that 'orientation to transcendental mystery' of which Lonergan has spoken and which he regards as the *sine qua non* of the theological quest?

Admittedly, the two kinds of transcendence, the human and the divine, do not precisely coincide. But here we may ask whether we should not revise our understanding of the divine transcendence in the light of the transcendence that we know directly in human experience. This human transcendence, as we have seen, is an intensely dynamic idea – it is the drive to go beyond. Has not our theological understanding of divine transcendence been, on the contrary, far too static? By the transcendence of God, we have understood primarily his otherness and distance from the created order. But what if the transcendence of God is also dynamic, the energy of the divine love thrusting out beyond, God's *exitus* into the world of the finite? Some such idea comes to expression in a striking passage in the writings of Denys. He says: 'And we must dare to affirm (for it is true) that the Creator of the universe himself, in his beautiful and good yearning towards the universe, is through the excessive yearning of his goodness transported out of himself in his providential activities towards all things that have being, and is touched by the sweet spell of goodness, love and yearning, and so is drawn from his transcendent throne above all things, to dwell in the heart of all things, through an ecstatic power that is above being and whereby he yet stays within himself.'[9] This is not the static transcendence of a lordly monarchical God, but the active transcendence of a God of love. It is therefore untouched by the objections of those philosophers who would say that a transcendent God is oppressive, and incompatible with the reality of human transcendence. On the contrary, the transcendence of God, understood in dynamic terms, is precisely his self-emptying (*kenosis*) and his coming to dwell at the heart of creation. Paradoxically, therefore, his transcendence coincides with his immanence, the supreme instance of the *coincidentia oppositorum*.

Another way in which the transcendence of the human being points to the mystery of God can be seen when we contemplate the natural world as a whole. As I have pointed out, the trend of thought for several centuries has been leading us in the direction of taking the world as something grounded in itself and needing no reality more ultimate than itself to account for it. If the natural world has this self-

completeness, then there is no God and even human transcendence is a limited inner-worldly phenomenon. But if
there is a reality more ultimate than nature and transcending
nature, then perhaps there is something in the world that
points to it. Surely it is the existence of humanity, the form
of being that has made a breach in nature through its
freedom, that does so point beyond the natural world. There
may be other mysteries even at the level of physical reality
that point beyond themselves, but we can never be sure
whether these are not simply gaps in our knowledge that will
eventually be filled in. Man alone seems to be the irreducible
mystery, the place where finite and infinite meet and so
the place where an orientation to transcendental mystery
becomes possible.

Let me express the point in still a third way. From ancient
times, the human being has been described as a microcosm.
He is so because he sums up in himself all the levels of being
that we can observe in the universe – the physico-chemical,
the organic, the sentient, the rational, the personal and whatever intermediate levels one might want to add. The idea of
the human being as a microcosm was taken just one step
further by Leibniz. In his view, a human being mirrors not
only the universe but, as gifted with mind and personality,
God himself in his relation to the world. 'Minds,' he declares,
'are also images of the deity or the author of nature himself,
capable of knowing the system of the universe and, to some
extent, of imitating it through their own inventions.'[10] So
Leibniz can say that each human being or spirit is like a 'little
god' in its own world. For this, of course, one may appeal
to the Bible, with its teaching that the first human couple
were made in 'the image and likeness of God' (Gen. 1.26).

So far, except for the very last sentence, I have been
moving in the area of natural theology. The whole claim
that man is the initial datum for theological reflection is
enormously strengthened when we turn to the Christian
revelation and specifically to the doctrine of incarnation. For
according to this teaching, God has made himself known in
and through a human person. We could on the one hand
say that in Jesus Christ humanity was brought to that level

of transcendence at which the image and likeness of God, obscured in our humanity through sin, has been brought to its full and explicit realization. I think this is what Dr Rahner had in mind when he stated, surely in a very strong form of words: 'Only someone who forgets that the essence of man . . . is to be unbounded . . . can suppose that it is impossible for there to be a man, who, precisely by being man in the fullest sense (which we never attain), is God's existence into the world.'[11] I think too that this is not far from Schleiermacher's description of Jesus Christ as the 'completion of the creation of man'.[12]

But something remains to be said. This is neither projection of the human image on an imaginary God nor is it a reduced and merely reductionist christology. Indeed, the antithesis between adoptionism and incarnationism is a false one. These two are complementary. A human being can manifest the being of God only because God himself has descended into the created order. There can be a divinity in man only because there is already a humanity in God. At this point we can pay Karl Barth his just due, but while he was right in affirming the ontological priority of God in this as in everything, and I would have no desire to differ from him on this point, it leaves unchanged my own contention that in the order of knowing, there is a legitimate and indeed compelling way that leads from the knowledge of the human to the knowledge of the divine.

Immediately after the lecture, Dr George Vass, formerly Professor of Dogmatic Theology at Heythrop, and now Professor at the theological faculty of Innsbruck, expressed on behalf of Dr Rahner (aware of the inadequacy of his spoken English), his warmest thanks to Professor Macquarrie and to Heythrop College for the honour paid to him. Having read the lecture beforehand, Dr Rahner had a comment to make, and three questions he would like to raise.

Dr Rahner's comment

I am in almost unreserved agreement with the main line taken by Professor Macquarrie, concerning the importance of an anthropological approach to theology. Above all, I agree with the underlining of the basic coherence or unity between, on the one hand, natural and revealed theology, and, on the other, apologetics and dogmatics. Of course, in this connection, I would not use the term 'apologetics' but rather 'fundamental theology'. I regard the latter not so much as a presentation of Christian dogma which should authenticate itself, but rather I would say that it is an *argumentative* effort of man in his approach to God. It is from this standpoint that I would like to raise the first of my questions.

Dr Rahner's first question

What reasons would Professor Macquarrie give on the basis of which he would hold that there is a coherence or indeed unity between natural and revealed theology? Would he agree that this coherence is based on the presupposition that *owing to the universal salvific will of God, everybody in his own freedom is challenged to a choice between the acceptance or the refusal of God's objectively offered grace?* If so, then does he agree that in our factual situation it is impossible to speak of a purely natural theology? Is not every man or woman standing under the effective call of God's revelation? From this it would follow that anyone who undertakes philosophical reflection today is confronted with a choice between the free acceptance or rejection of this existential grace of God, and his propositions must bear the signs of his choice. Would Professor Macquarrie agree that reasoning such as this supports his own position?

Reply by Professor Macquarrie

Well, I never thought I would have the honour of getting a *viva* from Dr Rahner . . . I may say that those of us who teach at Oxford try to make things a little easier. But I do not think there is any serious matter of disagreement here. There may be differences of terminology. I think I have always believed in what I might call a *common* grace: that creation itself brings with it a grace of creation; that as well as the specific Christian grace given in Jesus Christ there is a grace that is available for all human beings. So I would want to say at any rate that the border line between natural theology and Christian theology is a blurred one. Of course it is also the case that as far as those of us who have grown up in the Western world are concerned, there is a sense in which culturally speaking we cannot help being Christians. The Italian philosopher Benedetto Croce wrote an essay many years ago to which he gave the title, 'Why we cannot help calling ourselves Christians'. He meant that whatsoever our intellectual orientation might be, we had all heard the substance of the Christian faith, and therefore, it had become part of the intellectual environment in which we live. In that sense I suppose everyone is faced with the choice of either taking up this part of his heritage or setting it aside. So on the question, could there be a pure natural theology?, perhaps the answer is, 'No'; that almost inevitably overtones of Christianity would come in. On the other hand I think that natural theology is a good exercise. Fr Copleston and myself have both been up in Scotland in the last two or three years, where natural theology is one of the staple industries . . . due to the munificence of Lord Gifford who founded his Lectures back in the 1880s. And so we tried, so far as we could, to play according to the rules, in which we must not make appeal to what I think Lord Gifford called 'any special or miraculous revelation', but we had to treat our subjects as we might treat some secular subject. I think in a sense that is impossible. As I said in the course of the lecture, I do not think there can be any unaided knowledge of God, just as there can be no unaided knowledge of my neighbour; there has to be communication on a personal level. So I would say, I do not fundamentally disagree with the implications of the question: that it is the same God who addresses us in the specific Christian revelation, and (I think) in this wider, more general knowledge of himself which is given in and through the creation; and that the grace that we know in the Christian faith is continuous with a common grace, a grace of creation which is available to all human beings.

Dr Rahner's second question

There is a question I would like to raise about the teaching of Karl Barth: you mentioned his radical rejection of natural theology on the well-known ground that the (Catholic) principle of *analogia entis* is unacceptable. Would you claim that Barth maintained his objection (as formulated in his earlier writings), or that there came a slight change in his attitude, which eventually brought him closer to the classical Thomistic position? To adopt another formulation: given that God's grace and self-communication are always *a priori* at work in a man, then can one argue with Barth that any effort, or apparent effort, from the side of man to reach God must be regarded as sinful or even blasphemous? Need one conceive the problem in terms of God descending vertically from above to man below, of man ascending to God above, if God is already present below, at the very beginning of man's search, in the form of grace-with-man?

Reply by Professor Macquarrie

We are brought here to the question of whether Barth changed his mind: certainly he worked for a long time, and I think probably he did change his mind. The early theology, if we go back to the kind of things he was writing round about the end of the First World War, is certainly a theology of very stark divine transcendence: the difference between God and man is absolute, God (as Fr Vass says) works *vertically* from above, and the human being was virtually passive. Now it seems to me that Barth did not retreat from some of these basic views; I do not think he ever came to the point where he would be willing to accept even the kind of modified natural theology that I was speaking about, nor would he be able to accept that religion is other than a grasping at God. But nevertheless I think a change did come over his views in the 1960s, when he wrote his little book called *The Humanity of God*, and that of course was very much in line with the teaching in the second half of Volume 2 of his enormous *Dogmatics* (he almost rivals Dr Rahner in production . . .) In that particular part of his Dogmatics he speaks of God in the beginning of all his works and ways electing man as his covenant partner. Jesus Christ, the second Person of the Trinity, is already (shall we say) pre-existent from all eternity as a man, and God elects humanity, elects the whole of humanity, in Jesus Christ. So in that theology it is the case really that the human has been there in the mind and heart of God from the very beginning, and that this humanity is accepted and elected in Jesus Christ. Barth too is a universalist: he believes that the whole human race, whether it is conscious of it or not, is already elected in Jesus Christ.

Now when one begins to look at these questions, as so often in theology you see that what we are dealing with here is a dialectic, and the great mistake is to seize upon one side rather than the other and to push it to extremes. Barth sees that the initiative always comes from God: God is the creator, the originator, the saviour, the One with the 'salvific will' (to use Dr Rahner's expression), and so that all comes from God, and in that sense the human being himself is simply responding to what God has already offered and created and brought about. On the other hand of course, if we think of it from the human side, then in our way of knowing we begin by knowing human relationships and the human condition; it is only from that that we can form some analogical conception of what God is like, of what God is doing. I think it was Barth who said at one time that we do not know the fatherhood of God from our human fathers; it is rather that, if we are ever going to understand what human fatherhood is, it will only be in the light of what we know of the fatherhood of God. You can see that is true, or at least that it is half the truth, or maybe two thirds of the truth. . . But on the other hand, the word 'father' is a human word, and we can only attach any meaning to it because of our own human relationships. So while in the end the whole conception of fatherhood must be as it were purified, and elevated, and understood in its essence (shall we say) for the first time, when we know something about the fatherhood of God, nevertheless our minds begin from the human end. However poor or degraded human fatherhood may often be, in some minimal degree at least it mirrors the fatherhood of God.

Dr Rahner's third question

In a quite different area, I would like to raise a question about *the minimalizing of sin in modern society*. You have argued that it is no longer possible to point, as Barth did, to man's sinfulness as a reason for saying that he cannot approach God. Indeed, Barth's attempt to radicalize man's sinfulness achieves an effect contrary to the one he desired: it minimalizes and understates the seriousness of sin itself (for it suggests that in one's powerlessness against sin there is nothing worth trying). But while I agree that there is an unfortunate trend in modern society to minimalize sin, is this to be read simply as an indication of the basic godlessness of our contemporaries, or does it not rather imply the existence of an implicit awareness of a redemption already achieved and of a forgiveness granted by God? In other words, the problem felt by both Dr Vass and myself concerns the possibility for man of experiencing sin in its radical seriousness (as seen by God): only one man was able to see and experience the horrifying nature of sin, and this was Jesus Christ. Hence one final question: even in the modern minimalizing of sin, can one not see a sign of God's grace at work?

Reply by Professor Macquarrie

Clearly of course there could be a preoccupation with sin, and an unhealthy dwelling on the thought of sin which could be injurious. Really in a sense, as I think Fr Rahner is implying there, one has to hear the words, '*Your sins are forgiven*'. This is the great truth of the Christian religion: not that human beings are wretched and sinful, but rather that their sins are forgiven. I think it was Santayana who once said (rather a parody of Calvinism), that it is beautiful that God should exist, and that he should punish sinners. There is that sort of unhealthy preoccupation with sin. On the other hand you could also say that it is the awareness of sin that is the first step towards redemption from sin. It is only when people confess their sins, or recognize their sins, that they can turn towards repentance and renewal. Now it may be of course that sin at different times takes different forms. Paul Tillich made rather a good point when in his little book, *The Courage to Be*, he suggested that in the early days of the church people were primarily concerned about death and annihilation; then at the time of the Reformation, around the sixteenth and seventeenth centuries, there was the great concern for righteousness; he suggests that in modern times the threat to a great many human beings is really the threat of meaninglessness, that life seems to have been emptied of meaning. Of course these things are not mutually exclusive. The meaninglessness of modern life may to some extent be due to the sinfulness of human beings, both in the sense that they exploit one another and deprive one another of meaning, and perhaps also that their own desires and ambitions are of such a kind that they are bound to be frustrated.

I gather from Dr Rahner, from the question read out by Fr Vass, that Dr Rahner himself is not happy about the minimalizing of sin in the modern world, but there is perhaps one thing here where I feel a little bit uneasy, both with Dr Rahner and Dr Barth. Both of them, as I understand from their writings, take the view that the whole human race already is embraced by the salvific will of God, and that in a sense the decisive salvation has already taken place, although this has all got to work itself out in history. What I think worries me is the idea that human beings can somehow be already recipients of salvation and yet not be aware of it, that there can be as it were unconscious salvation. Certainly Karl Barth speaks often in that way. Yet it does seem to me that the human being is so much constituted by consciousness and responsibility and self-understanding (and so on), that the concept of salvation cannot really mean very much until he begins to understand it and appropriate it into his own being. That, I think, among other things would call for the recognition and confession of human sinfulness, and this is the beginning of a turning from it. I remember an exchange away back in the 1950s between Barth and Bultmann: it is in a small book of Karl

Barth called, 'Rudolf Bultmann: an attempt to understand him' (*ein Versuch ihn zu verstehen*). Barth's criticism of Bultmann at that time was that Bultmann, he thought, laid too much stress on the human decision and on the human acceptance of the Gospel. Barth's point was that whether human beings accept or do not accept, they are already elected in Jesus Christ, and whether or not they know it, they are already embraced by this saving act. I have some difficulties and reservations about that.

The meeting was brought to a close by the Principal of Heythrop College, Dr F. X. Walker, who took the opportunity of reading the text of a letter from Cardinal Basil Hume. The document deserves publication as the final piece – last but not least indeed – in the tribute offered to Dr Rahner on 17 February 1984.

Archbishop's House
Westminster
London SW1P 1QJ

Rev F. X. Walker, SJ,
Principal,
Heythrop College,
11 Cavendish Sq., London W1M 0AN   17 1 84

Dear Father Walker,
I regret very much that I have to be in Rome on February 17th and so I am unable to attend the Heythrop lecture in honour of Father Karl Rahner.

I am delighted that the College is able this evening to honour the eightieth birthday of a priest and scholar who has made such an outstanding contribution to theological thought in our time. I offer him in the name of Heythrop and on my own behalf our respect, our gratitude and our prayers.

I am certain that Dr Macquarrie's lecture will prove to be an entirely satisfying way of honouring our revered guest. The presence among you of two such men is a witness to the place that Heythrop College plays today in the life of the church in this country and in the academic world. There are difficulties always in maintaining such a role, but I am convinced that the sacrifices needed to sustain and develop the College and its work are entirely worthwhile.

May I ask you to convey to Fr Rahner, Dr Macquarrie and those assembled on February 17th my apologies for absence, my best wishes and blessing and my hope that your meeting will prove to be a thoroughly enjoyable occasion.

Yours devotedly,
Basil Hume,
Archbishop of Westminster

7

God in Experience and Argument

Philosophies of religion can be classified in many ways, but one of the most basic distinctions is between those which appeal to experience and those which base themselves on argument. Although I am going to maintain that finally each type needs the other, this is not obvious and there is no simple way of showing how the two types can be brought into relation with each other. To begin with, one is more aware of the differences between them. Philosophers who embrace the first type are often impatient of the second. They say that the philosophy of religion which proceeds by reasoning and argument has strayed far from the life of religion itself, that it deals in abstractions rather than with the concrete reality known in religion, and that it is in any case superfluous, for what proofs are needed by the person who has had first-hand experience of the religious reality and has known God face to face? Attempts to prove the validity of the experience (it is said) can lead only to bewilderment and uncertainty. On the other hand, philosophers who embrace the second type of theory may hold that theirs is the only correct approach *for philosophers*. Perhaps the religious person can get by on the basis of his religious experience alone, but the philosopher is committed to asking questions, seeking reasons, entertaining and discriminating among competing explanations. He knows that experience is sometimes deceptive, and he may think that the experiences of the religious person are so subjective that no truth claims can be established upon them. So he finds the appeal to experience unconvincing, and holds that if there is indeed a reality called God who is known in religion, this can be established only by a logical procedure which would develop a coherent concept of God and would then show that this concept refers to something real.

It is the second type of philosophy of religion that has the longer history. It was used in classical times, flourished in the Middle Ages and the Enlightenment, and has persisted down to modern times. In that long history, there have been many arguments and counter-arguments, and ever more subtle refinements of the opposing points of view. The first type of philosophy of religion, the type which appeals to experience, has been more typical of the modern age. Its rise may be due in part to the high value which we moderns accord to experience, since we all share something of the empirical temperament. On the other hand, it may be due in part to the fact that from the time of Hume and Kant the older arguments have been seen to have serious weaknesses, so that if one continues to practise religion and to believe in God, and if one is not content to do this simply on the authority of Bible, church or tradition, one looks for another ground than that provided by the classic theistic proofs. But it may be due in part also to the rise of modern individualism and to the demand for what is called 'personal' religion. Pascal is a good illustration of the shift from the rational argumentative type of philosophy of religion to the experiential type. Descartes is the philosopher whom Pascal has in mind in his criticisms, and Descartes is indeed a case where the philosophical approach to the problem of God seems at its most abstract. The existence of God is established by the most thoroughly rational of all the traditional arguments, the ontological argument, and the function of God in Cartesian philosophy seems to be chiefly that of guaranteeing the veracity of our knowledge of the external world. It is against such a background that we are to understand Pascal's famous words, 'God of Abraham, God of Isaac, God of Jacob, not of the philosophers and scholars'.[1] In another passage, he declares that 'the metaphysical proofs of God are so remote and complicated that they make little impression; and even when they are useful to some people, they are so only in that moment when their demonstrative force is perceived, but an hour later, the same people fear that they have been deceived'.[2] The separation of the God of faith from the God of metaphysics, the distrust of argument and the appeal to experience continue, though in different forms, in Schleiermacher, Kierkegaard, Ritschl and many other religious thinkers down to the present time.

Let us consider more closely the type of philosophy of religion that bases itself on an appeal to experience. It includes a variety of sub-types. In one form, the appeal is to distinctively religious experience, though this again is very diverse and includes worship, conversion, mysticism, spirit possession and so on. The appeal to distinctively religious experience is basic to the thought of Schleiermacher and Otto, and is believed by them to give assurance of the presence and reality of God or of the holy. But among more recent thinkers, the appeal is to a broader spectrum of experience. Perhaps it is even claimed that there is no distinctive *religious* experience, but that there is a religious dimension in many of our everyday experiences which would not be thought of as primarily religious. Here one might mention 1. self-experience, the basic experience of existing as a human person. This carries with it a sense of finitude, which might direct the person thus made aware of his fragmentariness to the search for a reality more stable and enduring than himself; though it also carries the sense of transcendence, the drive inherent in the human being to go beyond every state of himself toward a fuller being. Next one may mention 2. conscience. Though this may not be crudely equated with the voice of God, yet moral experience seems to many people to have a religious significance – as witness the many books that have been written on how the moral life finds its completion in religion. Of course, conscience may be experienced as condemning and as accusing of guilt, or it may be experienced as directing towards some course of action or some state of being, and both types of conscience can have religious significance. 3. Commitment, in its many forms, is still another type of experience that may have religious overtones. Here we are thinking of the more important commitments which a person takes upon himself or herself.

They confer identity on the person who accepts them, and form what Tillich felicitously called 'ultimate concern'. 4. In some persons of an intellectual cast of mind, the experience of order in the world has a religious character. The rationality of the human mind looks for a rationality in the world, and feels a sense of kinship when such rationality is discovered. There are scientists of whom this is true – Einstein, for instance, spoke of 'cosmic religion', meaning the faith that the universe is rationally ordered. Something similar is found in some philosophers; Bradley wrote that 'with certain persons, the intellectual effort to understand the universe is a principal way of thus experiencing the Deity' and that philosophy is 'a satisfaction of what may be called the mystical side of our nature'.[3] We may add 5. aesthetic experience. The beauty and harmony experienced by certain people in nature or in art has something of a religious character. Many of the romantic poets had a religious – albeit somewhat pantheistic – feeling for nature, while in the present secularized atmosphere of our culture many people seem to get some religious satisfaction from music or the visual arts. 6. Interpersonal relations constitute still another area where some people are sensitive to a religious dimension. In a deep relation to another person, the boundaries of self are transcended and this may have religious significance for some people or in some situations. We recall Buber's familiar words: 'Every particular "Thou" is a glimpse through to the eternal "Thou".'[4] Finally, 7. even suffering and death can have for some a definitely religious character. If there are those who think of suffering and death as destructive of meaning in human life, there are others who claim that they prevent them from trying to understand themselves within their own narrow individual being, so that they have to see themselves as part of a larger ongoing whole.

I have mentioned here seven areas of experience in which some people might claim to perceive a religious dimension, and no doubt the list could be expanded. We are not to forget, however, that before mentioning those seven areas where the religious element appears in, so to speak, a secondary way, I had already mentioned experiences which are primarily religious – worship, conversion and the like. Perhaps it is only because some people have those primary religious experiences that it is possible to perceive a religious dimension in the other kinds of experience I have mentioned. On the other hand, a person who said that he never had a religious experience and did not know what such an experience was like might be introduced to it if he could be persuaded to focus his attention on what are claimed to be the religious dimensions of, let us say, aesthetic or moral or interpersonal experience. Still, in casting the net so widely we have to be aware of a danger. If religious experience is so widely diffused through many different kinds of experience, does it not lose its distinctiveness and become something so vague and indeterminate that we cannot say anything worthwhile about it? I do not think this is the case, but I do take the point that the so-called religious dimension will have to be specified much more clearly if it is to be taken seriously.

If religious experience (or some other kind of experience having a religious dimension) is held to bring the person having the experience into an encounter with a divine or holy reality, then I do not think that the experience alone guarantees that such an encounter or meeting has taken place. It could reasonably be claimed, of course, that there is a *prima facie* case in religious experience as in any other experience that through the experience there takes place an encounter with a reality beyond the consciousness of the experiencing subject, but the experience cannot be held to be self-authenticating. All experience, even sense experience, is fallible. Sometimes people believe themselves to be seeing or hearing things that just aren't there. Since religious experience is neither as universal as sense experience nor as straightforwardly checkable, its testimony cannot be accepted without further ado. It is true of course that a devoutly religious person may have complete certitude that God has met him or spoken to him, so that anything further would seem to such a person not only superfluous but even verging on the blasphemous. Consider the famous words of

John Wesley about his conversion: 'I felt my heart strangely warmed, I felt I did trust in Christ . . . and an assurance was given me that he had taken away my sins . . . and that I testified openly to all there.'[5] No one denies that Wesley had the experience he describes, and perhaps there is even a *prima facie* case, as I have suggested, for believing that this was an encounter with God in Christ. But if this is challenged, something more is needed than just the testimony of Wesley, irrefutable though it may have seemed to him.

The first move, however, would not be to turn away from the experience and to try to substitute argument for it. It would be to explore the experience more fully. Experience does not come to us in complete rawness. It is more than sensation, though it includes sensation. Our experiences are already clothed in language, so that we can offer a description of the experience. Beyond the description, we often go on to offer an interpretation. In the example quoted, Wesley describes his experience in terms of a sensation of warmth, feelings of trust, assurance and forgiveness. And he interprets or explains the experience in terms of the action of Christ.

Thus to offer a careful description of an experience must be the first step towards evaluating it. It is such a description too that can enable other people to compare their experiences and ask whether they have known anything comparable to what is described. I think that any description either of a primary religious experience or of the religious dimension that is claimed to be present in other kinds of experience would draw attention to two basic characters – intentionality and ultimacy.

I mention first *intentionality*. It is the mark of religion that it draws a person out of himself or herself, that it relates him to a larger reality. It has always been understood, of course, that there is bad religion as well as good, illusory as well as true. No doubt there can be religion in which an experience is enjoyed for its own sake, as one might enjoy, let us say, drug experience. But the aim of religion is to link the life of the devotee with a life that is higher than his own. Religious experience by its very nature stretches out beyond the self of the individual believer. Indeed, to the religious person, what he encounters in faith is more real than anything else. It stands over against him, perhaps judging, perhaps supporting, but always other than himself – indeed, in some forms of religious experience, 'wholly other'. This intentionality, by which I mean the reference of the experience to a reality beyond the person who has the experience, is a basic characteristic of religious experience. Any interpretation will have to take it into account, and I should think that any interpretation which explained it away would be not so much an interpretation of religion as its abolition. But of this I shall say more in a moment.

Meanwhile I turn to *ultimacy*. By this I mean that in religious experience one strikes against the limits of all experience. This happens directly in such experiences as mysticism or the sense of the presence of God in worship, but it happens also in the various types of experience which I listed as having a religious dimension. Conscience, for instance, in many cases is simply the voice of society, the superego, shot through with the relativism of a particular culture or subculture. But the very fact that conscience can transcend and judge its cultural expressions, pointing beyond them to an ideal of humanity and community, indicates that it cannot be explained only in sociological terms. Or again, the sense of beauty and harmony that arises from some limited scene of nature or work of art points beyond itself to a universal form; the discovery of rationality in a limited area of the universe points to a rationality pervading the whole; the relation to another finite person suggests the relation to an 'eternal Thou' as the centre of a universal community – as Teilhard de Chardin expressed it, the 'creatures are not merely so linked together in solidarity that none can exist except all the rest surround it, but all are so dependent on a single central reality that a true life, borne in common among them all, gives them ultimately their consistence and their unity'.[6] This, then, is the kind of ultimacy that I have in mind as a basic character of religious experience – a pointing beyond the immediate and the relative to the limits, to the deepest reality which embraces and transcends all finite realities.

Description then yields these two basic characteristics of religious experience – intentionality and ultimacy. Any interpretation that seeks to be plausible must take these characteristics with utmost seriousness. It seems to me that theism is the interpretation that does most justice to the data revealed in the phenomenology of religious experience. A well-constructed coherent theism is the most adequate and satisfying way of accounting for those experiences of intentionality and ultimacy which lie at the very foundation of religion.

The alternative, I suppose, is some reductionist explanation of religion, where 'God' is taken to be a veiled and misleading way of referring to society or humanity or something of the sort. It is always possible that the reductionist account is true, and that the elements of intentionality and ultimacy in religious experience are illusory. But here I think one might claim that the theistic explanation is more adequate than the reductionist accounts, not least because it gives a straightforward interpretation of the data and is not involved in ingenious attempts to show that things are other than they seem. But what is probably the least satisfactory account of all in the matter of religious experience is the view that tries to hold on to the value of religion while frankly embracing a reductionist explanation – I have in mind Dewey's 'common faith', Maslow's 'peak experiences', and the like. For when religion has been deprived of intentionality and ultimacy, the experience has been changed, it is no longer religion but, as I said before, something like a drug experience. For true religion liberates the devotee into a reality larger than himself and is never a sensation to be privately enjoyed. That is why the higher religions have always been closely associated with the life of moral striving and why conversion does not lead to a desire for more experiences but is typically followed by a sense of being called to service in the world.

Up to this point, we have seen that a philosophy of religion that begins from the side of experience can advance quite a long way, whether it begins from specifically religious experience or takes the wider view that 'religious experience is ordinary experience controlled by religious selectivity and interpretation'.[7] Yet we have also had to acknowledge that in the end it may be illusion. Furthermore, we have passed over the fact that for some people experience points to the absence of God rather than to his presence. While atheism often arises from a logical critique of religion, there is also an atheism that arises from experience. There is therefore a parallel between the two types of philosophy of religion, experiential and argumentative, and two types of atheism, which may be similarly designated. This was made very clear during the debates over the 'death of God' in the 1960s. Some of the new atheists of that time passionately denied God on the basis of an experience of godlessness. Because their denial had this passionate and experiential quality, we could say that the God whom they denied was the God of Abraham, Isaac and Jacob, the God known in the history of faith. An obvious exemplar of this kind of atheism was Richard Rubenstein, and he made his denial on the basis of the Jewish experience, especially the experience of Auschwitz and the attempted genocide carried out by the Nazis. Very different is the kind of atheism encountered in Paul van Buren's writings of the same period, for what troubled him was the alleged incoherence of God-language. The God whom he denied was primarily the God of the philosophers, the concept of a transcendent being.

We must then acknowledge that experience alone, even though it may seem overwhelmingly convincing to the person who has had some signally revealing experience (whether it has revealed God or the absence of God), and even although it can be refined and made more intelligible through description and interpretation, must still leave us with a question mark. Although the starting point that lies in experiences seems so different from the one that lies in intellectual speculation, the more we explore experience, the more we seem to be driven towards the rational activities of analysis, discrimination, validation. This happens especially when we come to the vital question of interpreting experience and in trying to account for it in terms of realities beyond the experiencing subject. I should add, however, that perhaps this language of an experiencing 'subject' is not very happy. Certainly, it is misleading if it suggests that there is an isolated subject who enjoys or undergoes his experiences in himself, and that this subject has somehow to be subsequently related to entities beyond himself. It is only if one sets out from such presuppositions that the claim that religious experience (or some other kind of experience) is 'subjective', in the sense that it refers to nothing that exists independently of my own stream of consciousness, comes to be made. On the contrary, it has to be contended that the so-called 'subject' of experience is always, in Heidegger's significant expression, a 'being-in-the-world'. He begins 'out there', so to speak, and it is superfluous to attempt to prove the 'reality of the external world'. Even our most private feelings, such as Wesley's sense of warmth, his trust and assurance, and so on, are registers or indexes of a situation in which he is one item among others,[8] and that is why such feelings are always strongly intentional. Even so, I come back to the point that the description and interpretation of religious experience leads more and more into the area of the exercise of reason and judgment. In spite of the apparently wide gulf separating the way of experience from the way of argument, it begins to be apparent that we could have much more assurance about the results to which the former of these ways leads if the second way were found to provide an independent route to the same destination.

So now we turn to the second of our two types of philosophy of religion, the type that proceeds by way of argument. As with the other type, one may distinguish subtypes. First among these is the purely rational approach, which proceeds simply by considering and analysing concepts already present to the mind, prior to any experience. The most celebrated case is the 'ontological proof' of God's existence. If it is acknowledged that the mind has the concept of a being free from the limitations and imperfections that belong to ordinary finite beings, then, it is argued, one is compelled to go on to assert the reality of such a being – ' a being than whom no greater can be conceived', in Anselm's language. On the other hand, it may be found impossible to construct a coherent concept of such a being, and in that case the ontological proof would turn to an ontological disproof of God's existence. This purely rational consideration of the concept of God might seem to be at the furthest remove from the God of religious experience – the present writer never came nearer to being persuaded of the absolute disjunction between the God of faith and the God of the philosophers than on the occasion of spending a day with a group of philosophers discussing the ontological argument! Yet however abstract the concept of God might be and however it might be manipulated in argument, the very fact that such a concept is, in the traditional language, 'innate' to the human mind is a fact of religious significance. If this concept can be given a coherent shape, this would not (in my view) prove the reality of God, but it would mean that 'God' has to be taken very seriously, and it would clearly strengthen that interpretation of religious experience which holds that it arises from the impinging of a divine reality upon us. More common, however, than the purely rational arguments are those which introduce an empirical element. The word 'empirical' should not mislead us here, for there is not an appeal to experience in the same way as with philosophies of religion that seek to base themselves on religious experience. In the present case, the arguments have an empirical element only in the sense that they draw upon evidences taken from our observation of the world, and seek to deduce the reality of God from these evidences. Here we have in mind such traditional proofs or arguments as those based on causality and on the alleged evidences of purpose in the universe. Even these arguments might seem once more to be very remote from the religious concern with God. What have a First Cause or an Unmoved Mover or a Supreme Intelligence or a Necessary Being to do with the God of Abraham, Isaac and Jacob or with the God who was incarnate in Christ? But again, these ways of thinking about God may not be at an infinite remove from each other. Is it something like a religious interest, namely, the quest to

understand man's place in the scheme of things, that motiv-
ates inquiries into the nature of reality, however abstract and
logically rigorous these may be? While, on the other hand,
might it not be claimed that the religious experience of God
and the very act of worshipping and adoring him entail that
he includes such notions as First Cause, Necessary Being,
Supreme Intelligence and the like, though the average
worshipper would probably be unaware that such descriptions are implicit in the very act of naming God? Again, just
as the way that leads from experience needs confirmation
from the independent way that proceeds by argument (*fides
quaerens intellectum*), so the abstractions of speculations are
fleshed out when the arguments are related to experience.
The arguments themselves are inconclusive, but are they not
strengthened when people report experiencing a God who
is in recognizable relation to the being demanded by the
arguments?

I agree with James Richmond that it is a mistake to separate
too sharply the God of religion from the God of philosophy.
He writes: 'When the term "God" is fully and thoroughly
unpacked, vital meanings are discerned which might be
overlooked if the unpacking were carried out only in the
light of the immediate needs of individual piety and commitment . . . God is indeed the "being whom we set our heart
and trust upon", but he is that precisely because he is the
transcendent and creative ground of the finite world and all
that it contains.'[9] We could put it in another way by saying
that every belief that we hold, when we subject it to scrutiny,
has both a history in our experience and a grounding in our
rationality. In the case of religious beliefs, especially the
fundamental belief in God, the experience comes first. Then
follows the argument, which may either confirm the
interpretation of the experience or, in the case of some
people, fail to do so. Thus the two ways which in their
beginning were so different finally converge.

8

The Idea of a Theology of Nature

Daniel Day Williams used often to say that most Christian theology of recent times lacks any treatment of nature as a theological theme. Unquestionably there is justice in this complaint.

Williams believed that the main reason for this lack was to be found in the preoccupation of twentieth-century theologians with categories that have driven it more and more in the direction of subjectivism or, at least, with the life of the human person. Thus Barth was concerned with revelation, Brunner with personal encounter, Bultmann with existentialism, and so on. Of course, all this is understandable, since faith itself touches on human life in its depth and inwardness. All of the theologians mentioned brought great gains to their subject by their chosen methods, yet it could well be argued that there were losses as well, for inevitably every theological method pays for its insights in some areas with its insensitivity in others.

Although a theology of nature is not a natural theology in the traditional sense of that expression, there is sufficient affinity between the two for it to be likely that the sharp rejection of natural theology by Barth, Brunner, Bultmann and many others of their generation made it virtually impossible for them from the very outset to develop any theology of nature. But the weakness has in fact characterized Protestant theology for a very long time – ever since Schleiermacher, the father of modern Protestant theology, shifted the focus of inquiry to the inner religious experience of the believer, to the latter's sense and taste for the infinite and his feeling of absolute dependence, his God-consciousness, or however it might be described. There were some protests in the nineteenth century, mostly half-hearted and ineffectual. Ritschl, for instance, wrote that 'three points are necessary to determine the circle by which a religion is completely represented – God, man and the world'.[1] He claimed that in German theology since Schleiermacher the third of these points has been omitted or minimized. Though subsequent theologians may have diverged from Schleiermacher in many ways, 'in one respect his precedent dominates them, namely, in the fact that religion is always represented simply as a relation to God, and not at the same time as a relation of man to the world'.[2] In fact, Ritschl's own preoccupation with ethics meant that he himself paid little attention to the world *as nature*, and even Barth in spite of all his criticisms of Schleiermacher remained enmeshed in the toils of a theology which speaks of the God-human relationship (theanthropology, as Barth came to call it) and has little to say of the world as such.

But the reasons for the neglect of nature by theologians can be traced much further back than the theologies of the past two hundred years. The truth is that the very idea of 'Nature'[3] is foreign to the Bible and so to any theology which draws its categories primarily from the Bible. The Bible has no word corresponding to 'Nature' in the broad inclusive sense. Instead, if the Bible wishes to speak of the totality of finite and physical entities, it speaks of the 'creation', and this word carries with it connotations quite different from those that come to mind when we use the word 'Nature'. The language of creation sees the world as having only a secondary and dependent reality. It is the product of God's creative will and comes to be regarded as little more than the stage on which human history is to be played. Hence, as we often hear, it is history and not Nature that provides the basic concepts for the biblical writers.

The word 'nature' has many meanings, but in the sense with which we are concerned here, 'Nature' stands for an order or power immanent in and at work in the physical universe. Whereas creation, in orthodox Christian theology, is the passive product of the divine will, Nature is active and originating and its relation to God may be left ambiguous. It is significant that it was around the time of the Renaissance, just when modern science was beginning to develop and Christian faith was beginning to be called in question that talk of Nature as an active principle (a kind of substitute for God) becomes common in European writers. *The Oxford English Dictionary* gives interesting examples from the sixteenth century in which we hear of Nature 'making', 'appointing', and so on. Nature has here a measure of autonomy which did not belong to creation. It is *Natura naturans*. Furthermore, Nature comes to be regarded as a mother. The religion of Nature, so rigorously expelled by the prophetic and historical emphases of the Old Testament, begins to reappear first in the neo-paganism of the Renaissance and then later in Romanticism. And at the same time the feminine principle begins to reassert itself. In Schiller's great *Ode to Joy*, human beings are represented as nourishing themselves at the breasts of nature.

Already in the eighteenth and more definitely in the nineteenth century new and somewhat sinister characteristics were beginning to attach themselves to Nature. Especially with the rise of the theory of evolution, the human race itself came to be seen as a product of Nature and a part of Nature. Whereas in the biblical conception of the creation Adam and Eve with their descendants had dominion over the earth, in the new way of understanding matters human beings were themselves but a transient product of Nature, perhaps owing their existence only to random events in Nature. So the face of Nature was changing. The benevolent motherly features faded and were replaced by an impersonal mask behind which lay the mechanistic uncaring universe of nineteenth-century physics. The idea of Nature's wisdom in making and appointing had been superseded by the chilling suspicion that she operates blindly and without knowledge, and that all things, ourselves included, have their origin in chance and necessity. Nature had by now become a self-regulating system governed by its own 'great eternal iron laws'. This phrase is taken from Ernst Haeckel's book, *The Riddle of the Universe*, an immensely popular handbook of the new scientific understanding of the world, published just at the end of the nineteenth century. There is no longer any room for God in such a scheme, for Nature is itself the ultimate reality. If there were a God, he too would be a product of Nature. As Haeckel sarcastically put it, the God of the Bible would have to be conceived in modern terms as 'a gaseous vertebrate'. Nineteenth-century biologists had compounded the picture by representing the evolutionary process as a cruel unrelenting struggle – 'Nature red in tooth and claw'. Nature, the wise mother and loving goddess who had emerged briefly from the time from the Renaissance to the age of the Romantics, seemed to have been lost, to be replaced by a faceless Nature of rigidly determined particles, a Nature going blindly and unconsciously on its way, causing enormous suffering as it did so and utterly regardless of the human race that had been accidentally thrown up in its midst.

It is not surprising that for a long time the term 'naturalism' was used for a type of philosophy which was quite reductionist in its tendency and had no place for such concepts as God, spirit and freedom.

But human thought does not stand still. Almost a century after Haeckel, we find ourselves in a situation where the understanding of Nature has changed again. That world of hard massy particles mechanistically determined to all eternity has vanished like a bad dream. Its 'atoms' have turned out to be not really 'atoms' (indivisible particles) but more like Chinese boxes which, as each one is opened, seem to bring us into a universe possessing an intricacy, a mystery and yet an openness all undreamed of in the nineteenth century. As the physicist Harold K. Schilling has written, 'The more we learn about nature, the less we need fear it and the more we can trust it and enter with joyous expectancy into its life and further development.'[4] There has been an equally dramatic change in the way biologists understand the living world and its evolution. Whereas the nineteenth century thought in terms of cruel incessant struggle, the twentieth century is more impressed with the organic interrelatedness and interdependence of all living things. The new understanding is far more compatible with a religious interpretation. 'The astonishing thing about our deepened understanding of reality as it has developed over the last four or five decades,' write Barbara Ward and René Dubos, 'is the degree to which it confirms so many of the older moral insights of man.'[5]

Thus 'naturalism' need no longer be a bad word in the ear of the theologian and it need not carry reductionist connotations. As Daniel Williams himself wrote, 'It makes a great deal of difference whether or not you mean pre-twentieth-century naturalism or contemporary naturalism.'[6] He himself found Whitehead's interpretation of Nature in the light of recent science rich enough to allow room both for God and for the human spirit.

I would like to suggest, however, that the interpretation of Nature offered by Whiteheadian philosophers and theologians, taking its rise from the picture presented by the contemporary natural sciences and so working, as it were, from below upwards towards a unifying philosophy of Nature, can and perhaps should be supplemented by an alternative approach which moves in the opposite direction. I doubt whether the two approaches can be combined or synthesized, but I think they can correct and supplement each other. This alternative approach works from above downwards, and we find hints of it in some of the existentialist philosophers. Thus, although Williams was right to castigate existentialist and personalist theologians for their neglect of Nature, they might have been able to develop a more adequate theology of Nature if they had paid attention to some admittedly obscure clues in some of the existentialist writers by whom they were influenced.

I shall choose Martin Heidegger as an exemplar of a thinker who made some tentative moves towards developing a concept of Nature, and this concept shows some interesting and unusual features, arising from its existentialist roots. Admittedly, the existentialist has usually been concerned to stress the difference between man and Nature, precisely to defend our understanding of the human reality from the dangers of reductionism. But Heidegger thinks it is rather the human being that may yield the clue to understanding the non-human entities of Nature. The unspoken assumption seems to be close to the ancient view that the human being is a microcosmos, a mirror in miniature of the entire range of being manifested in the cosmos.

In his major early work, *Being and Time*, Heidegger divides inanimate things into two great categories – that which is present-at-hand (*vorhanden*) and that which is ready-to-hand (*zuhanden*). The present-at-hand includes the 'things of Nature' (*Naturdinge*) and to be merely present-at-hand means that whatever is so described simply occurs in this world and is not (or is not yet) experienced as having any relevance to human life. The ready-to-hand, by contrast, includes all the things that have in one way or another been related to the practical concerns of human life. Anything which is ready-to-hand has been incorporated into the world of human instrumentality and receives a meaning in terms of its function there.

The division between present-at-hand and ready-to-hand does not coincide with the division between naturally occurring objects and human artefacts, though it approximates to this division. But the things of Nature may themselves, without ceasing to be things of Nature, become ready-to-hand as human beings learn to use them for the satisfaction of needs or the realization of projects. For instance, even the stars become ready-to-hand in the sense that they may be used as markers for finding the way.

At this stage in his philosophizing, Heidegger seems to have envisaged man as engaged in the progressive humanization of the world. That is to say, more and more of the things of Nature are to be incorporated into the instrumental system. The river becomes a means for transportation and communication, the mountain becomes a quarry, even the wilderness may be preserved as wilderness for the sake of human needs and recreation. Thus, even the conservation of wild Nature in a national park is, paradoxically, the humanization of Nature. All of this does in fact lead in the direction of an anthropocentric philosophy which fits in very well with the modern drive toward unlimited technological expansion. The goal would be an entirely man-made and man-controlled environment in which nothing would be any longer merely present-at-hand. Everything would be ready-to-hand and would derive its meaning from its place in the dynamics of human concern.

However, there are a few hints of another point of view, even as early as *Being and Time*. It is this other point of view that has become more prominent in Heidegger's later philosophy and it has of course gained in importance as the ambiguities of technological advance and humanization of the environment have become clearer. In this new phase of his philosophy, we meet something that is at least suggestive of a more adequate philosophy of Nature, though one that would still have existential roots.

I have mentioned that there are already hints of this alternative view in *Being and Time*. One of these hints is found in Heidegger's brief reference to the ontological status of living beings other than men and women. They belong to an intermediate realm between *Dasein* (human existence) and physical Nature. How can we arrive at some understanding of these living beings or how do we gain access to the kind of being that belongs to an animal or plant? Heidegger does not think that an adequate understanding of the living can be gained from the side of the present-at-hand, that is to say, in terms of physics and chemistry. The existence of the human person, though it is that of a person rather than of an animal or plant, is nevertheless at one level *also* a living organism. Heidegger writes: 'Life, in its own right, is a kind of being; but its essence is accessible only in man. The ontology of life is accomplished by way of a privative interpretation; it determines what must be the case if there is anything like mere aliveness.'[7] Although Heidegger does not go on to work this out in detail, it is clear what he has in mind. Living creatures are not to be understood in reductionist fashion in terms of lower levels of being. They are to be understood by stripping down the higher (personal) levels till one comes to 'mere aliveness', and access lies through the human existent who has the immediate experience of what it means to be alive. But he does not have this experience as one of 'mere aliveness', for the biological levels of his being have been fused with or assumed into the personal level, and that is why there is demanded a 'privative' interpretation, an interpretation which would abstract from the full experience in order to reach the biological level.

Although in the passage we have discussed Heidegger was referring to living beings, the approach he suggests is a feasible one in considering Nature in its entirety. We do indeed find something quite similar in the British philosopher John Macmurray, who had many affinities with the existentialists. Macmurray points out that in the history of Western philosophy, personal being has frequently been interpreted in terms of lower levels of being, that is to say, in a reductionist manner. The doctrine of a soul-substance or *res cogitans* tried to understand spiritual or mental being on the model of substantiality or thinghood – a most inadequate model. With the rise of biology, an attempt was made to elucidate personhood on the model of a living organism. This was a step in the right direction, but the model was still inadequate. Persons cannot be understood as anything less than persons. But Macmurray claimed (and it is at this point that his thinking is very close to Heidegger's) that even organisms and substances are best grasped if we begin from what we know in ourselves as persons, and work *down* from there rather than trying to work *up*. Man is, so to speak, a multidimensional or many-levelled being (microcosmos) who gathers up into a complex unity all the lower levels. Thus Macmurray claims that it is in the human being that we have access to the meaning not only of personhood but of life and even substantiality.

How might a scientist be expected to react to such ideas? We should note in the first instance that Macmurray is interested in the philosophical or ontological elucidation of the ideas of organism and substance, not in the detailed empirical investigation of actual organisms and substances, such as natural scientists carry out. But even so, it is interesting to note the following words of the scientist John Habgood. They seem highly compatible with the suggestions of Heidegger and Macmurray, though they were made without any reference to these philosophers: 'We can ask physical and chemical questions [about a complete living creature] . . . but what is it to understand an animal as *a living creature*? I believe it means to recognize that it has a certain kinship with ourselves; that we belong to the same family.'[8]

One's whole conception of Nature may be profoundly influenced by the choice between the approach from below up and the approach from above down. Perhaps either approach in isolation will lead to a distorted view. The approach from below up, which has been the common one in the West in recent times, is almost inevitably reductionist, and at its worst resulted in the nineteenth-century concept of a mechanistically determined Nature. The approach from above down, in isolation, might have less injurious results, but it could well lead into merely romantic and even animistic attitudes to Nature. This is why it seems desirable to let the two approaches interact in a dialectical relation. Only so could one hope to be doing justice to the enormous complexity of Nature, taking into account both its personal and impersonal constituents, to say nothing of its aesthetic as well as its physical properties. And perhaps only so can we arrive at that right balance of manipulation and appreciation which seems to be demanded if the human race is to live in a healthy relation with environing Nature.

There is another interesting insight to be drawn from Heidegger. In several of his later writings he considers the meaning of *phusis*, the Greek term which is commonly translated as 'nature'.[9] Heidegger has a very dynamic interpretation of *phusis*, far removed indeed from Haeckel's 'great eternal iron laws'. For Heidegger, *phusis* is 'emerging', *entstehen*, 'standing out', even 'coming to light', for he tries to associate the words *'phusis'* and *'phos'* (light). The interesting point about these remarks is that now not only living things but the entire *phusis* is being seen privatively from the human end. Man, in Heidegger's view, *exists* or stands out, in a process of transcendence; but Nature, too, *entsteht* or stands out, as if it has the potentialities which have fulfilled themselves and come to speech in Nature's most amazing child.

Heidegger's words are worth quoting at some length. After

saying that *phusis* is 'emerging', and giving as instances the rising of the sun, the growth of plants and the coming forth of animals from the womb, he says: 'The Greeks did not learn what *phusis* is through natural phenomena, but the other way round; it was through a fundamental poetic and intellectual experience of Being that they discovered what they had to call *phusis*. Hence *phusis* originally encompassed heaven as well as earth, the animal as well as man, and it encompassed human history as a work of man and the gods; and first and last it meant the gods themselves as subordinated to destiny. *Phusis* means the power that emerges and the enduring realm under its sway.'[10]

In Heidegger's philosophy, which goes far beyond a mere 'existentialism', man and nature are not left in an irreconcilable dualism, as happens with Sartre. Rather, *Dasein* provides the clue to *phusis*. Admittedly, we do not have here a theology of Nature or even a fully elaborated philosophy of Nature. It is not a theology of Nature, for Heidegger embraces neither theism nor atheism. There are obvious religious overtones in what he says about *phusis*, but these have their ambience in Greek rather than in biblical religion. But perhaps there is a way from Heidegger's remarks towards a theology of Nature. I do not think that way could lead to the God of classical theism, conceived as another being beyond Nature, a monarchical deity who by an act of will creates Nature as something quite external to himself. Yet the way would not lead to atheism or to an impersonal Nature as the ultimate reality. But it could easily make contact with the Christian theology of someone like John Scotus Eriguena who used the word 'Nature' in the same broad sense as Heidegger, so that it includes both the human and the divine.

Much remains to be done towards working out a theology of Nature, but Heidegger's way towards the subject ensures that the human existent rather than the hydrogen atom is the starting place and the significant clue, and so any merely reductionist, or mechanistic way of conceiving Nature is ruled out from the beginning.

9

The Anglican
Theological Tradition

Is there such a thing as an Anglican theological tradition? I
believe that there is, but it is hard to define, and so there is
some excuse for those critics who say that Anglicanism has
no distinctive theology and that on doctrinal matters
'anything goes' within the Anglican communion.

It is, of course, true that there are no detailed statements
of an Anglican doctrinal position comparable either to the
dogmas and other authoritative pronouncements received
by the Roman Catholic Church and conveniently collected
in Denzinger's *Enchiridion Symbolorum* or to the many
'confessions of faith' put out by the various Protestant bodies
at the time of the Reformation and the subsequent period
and each stating a distinctive denominational position.
Anglicans have not felt it incumbent on them to spell out
doctrine quite so explicitly. This may be partly due to the
fact that they have never thought of themselves as separating
from the catholic church, and so it has been maintained that
Anglican doctrine is simply the doctrine of the whole church,
not that of some particular tradition. To some, this might
seem an arrogant claim, but it appears to receive some recognition in the decree on ecumenism of Vatican II, where it
is stated that among the communions stemming from the
Reformation, 'the Anglican communion occupies a special
place', because of its retention of catholic traditions and institutions.[1] However, it may be that the absence in Anglicanism
of detailed doctrinal statements is due quite as much to the
somewhat empirical and pragmatic temper of the English

people. In modern times, at any rate, there has been a distrust of over-precision in doctrinal matters and a recognition that theological statements are bound to have a more or less provisional character. The hesitation in the face of attempts at doctrinal formulation is evidenced not only in the official attitude of Anglicanism but also by the fact that few individual Anglican theologians have engaged in systematic theology. They have tended to be suspicious of 'systems', thinking perhaps that they are intellectually too ambitious or that they prematurely 'freeze' Christian truth in propositional form, so preventing further exploration. That this fear is quite unfounded may easily be seen by reading the works of continental dogmaticians, both Catholic and Protestant. Schleiermacher and Rahner are good illustrations of men who have not shirked the problems of systematic theology but have clearly recognized the provisional character of their undertaking.

But while the majority of Anglicans have been happy to refrain from close dogmatic definition, it does not follow that there is no recognizable Anglican position in theology nor even a distinctively Anglican way of going about the theological task. For instance, just by belonging to the World Council of Churches, the Church of England declares itself to be a church that believes in the Triune God. It may in fact contain theologians who do not so believe, but this is a testimony to the remarkable freedom and tolerance in matters theological enjoyed within the Church of England, and cannot be interpreted as meaning that unitarianism has the same status as trinitarianism in this church. The individual theologian has distanced himself in certain matters from the teaching of his church. The church – for good reasons – does not disown him, but neither does it endorse his teaching, for in its own daily liturgy it continues to proclaim its trinitarian faith.

From time to time, however, Anglicans are forced to be more forthcoming about where they stand in matters of theological belief. One of the most fruitful occasions on which this happened was in the inter-war years – I mean the setting up by the Archbishops of Canterbury and York in 1922 of a

Commission on Christian Doctrine, whose report, *Doctrine in the Church of England*, was published in 1938. The occasion for the setting up of this commission was the general feeling that World War I had ended an era and that the church must address itself to the question of how to express its beliefs in the strange new world of the twentieth century. There were more specific spurs to reflection. The Lambeth Conference of 1920 had opened up serious ecumenical discussions, and it was necessary for the Church of England to define its position in relation to other bodies with whom it might find itself in conversation. Again, there was considerable party strife in the church, with rather extreme sacramentalist views being put forward by the Anglo-Catholic Congress on the one hand and a minimizing christology by the Modern Churchmen's Union on the other. A good deal of pressure had to be put on the Archbishop of Canterbury (at that time Randall Davidson) before he agreed to the appointment of the commission. He was prey to the common Anglican anxiety that definition of doctrine is unnecessary and likely to be divisive, and Davidson's concern was chiefly to keep the boat from rocking. However, the commission was in fact appointed, and it is interesting to note its terms of reference: 'To consider the nature and grounds of Christian doctrine with a view to demonstrating the extent of existing agreement within the Church of England and with a view to investigating how far it is possible to remove or diminish existing differences.'[2] These words imply that the business of the commission was to present a factual report on what is actually believed in the church rather than a normative statement of the church's official belief. But in the actual report, there is inevitably some blurring of the distinction between these two different types of statement. The aim was to appoint to the commission younger theologians representing the main traditions in the church, and to allow them ten to twenty years for carrying out their task. Of the twenty-five members all were male, twenty-one were clergy and all except one were products of Oxford or Cambridge. The chairman was Bishop Burge, of Oxford, but he died in the early stages and was succeeded by the Bishop of Manchester, at that time William Temple.

Though its authors made only modest claims for it and though it aroused criticism among many who felt it went too far in acknowledging the legitimacy of a measure of pluralism in matters of doctrine within Anglicanism, the most competent judges have agreed that the report of 1938 is of its kind masterly. More than fifty years after its appearance, one still finds it quoted by Anglican participants in ecumenical dialogues as representing the position of their communion. It was reprinted in 1982 with an extensive introduction by Geoffrey Lampe, which he concluded by quoting as 'words that remain true' the comment made by a former Bishop of Manchester in 1938: 'It will be for a very long while a book which will help those who study it to reassert the faith and to exercise considerateness in so doing, and at the same time to preserve that freedom of thought and inquiry which has always been part of the Anglican tradition.'[3] It is, of course, true that a document composed in the early part of our century cannot answer all the questions being asked at its close. Yet it is also true that in theology the same questions keep coming back, even if in altered form. Thus Geoffrey Lampe points out that most of the arguments over christology aroused by the book called *The Myth of God Incarnate* (1978) had been anticipated in the controversy initiated by the Modern Churchmen's Union in the events that led up to the appointment of the Archbishops' Commission on Doctrine in 1922, while the ecumenical discussions over church, ministry and sacraments still centre on issues that are admirably treated, from an Anglican point of view, in the document of 1938.

In the report itself, after a brief introduction, something is said about the sources of Christian doctrine. Pride of place is given to scripture, and this is surely true to the Anglican tradition. But the doctrine of the verbal inerrancy of scripture is explicitly denied, and the writers make it clear that for them recognition of the authority of scripture is by no means incompatible with a critical approach. Next, the church is mentioned as a source of doctrine, and again it is true to the

Anglican tradition to allow a place to tradition alongside that of scripture. We read: 'All Christians are bound to allow very high authority to doctrines which the Church has been generally united in teaching; for each believer has a limited range, and the basis of the Church's belief is far wider than that of his own can ever be. An individual Christian who rejects any part of that belief is guilty of presumption, unless he feels himself bound in conscience to do so and has substantial reasons for holding that what he rejects is not essential to the truth and value of Christianity.'[4] The main body of the report falls into three parts: the first is on the doctrines of God and redemption; the second on the church and sacraments; the third on eschatology. One can hardly fail to be struck by the disproportion in length of these three parts. The section on church, ministry and sacraments gets more space than the other two put together – 102 pages, as against 58 for God and redemption and a mere 18 for eschatology! We shall later see something of the reason for this Anglican preoccupation with ecclesiology, but we can see that it gives some support to the gibe that one can be a good Anglican if one believes in episcopacy, no matter how much else one disbelieves!

In 1978 there appeared a timely book by Stephen Sykes, entitled *The Integrity of Anglicanism*. Sykes made the straight-forward claim that, in spite of all the waffling, 'the present Anglican church has incorporated a regular doctrinal structure in the content of its liturgy and in the rules governing its public performance'.[5] This point, by the way, was rather similar to one expressed by an Advisory Committee of the American Church, on which I had served myself. This committee had been appointed at the beginning of 1967 by the then Presiding Bishop (John E. Hines) to advise on the theological situation that had arisen out of some of the rather far out utterances of Bishop James Pike, and the threat by some of his fellow bishops to prosecute him for heresy. Perhaps, as in England more than forty years earlier, the main concern of the church leaders was to defuse the situation and avoid the adverse publicity that would have been caused by any heresy trial. Nevertheless, the deliberations of the committee were very useful, and led to the publication of the report entitled *Theological Freedom and Social Responsibility*. This document gave encouragement to theological speculation and disclaimed any wish to 'uphold a narrow verbal orthodoxy which requires a person to give literal assent to some particular formulation of doctrine', but went on to say: 'We do believe that if an individual finds himself unable, in good conscience, to identify with the living tradition of the church, reflected in the Bible, the creeds, and, especially for Anglicans, in the liturgy of the Book of Common Prayer, he should as a matter of personal integrity voluntarily remove himself from any position in which he might be taken to be an official spokesman for the whole community.'[6] So in both the passages quoted, the liturgy and the way of doing it is seen as decisive. There may be no documents which spell out precisely the content of Anglican belief in the form of a confession of faith, but what people do is sometimes better evidence of their inward beliefs than what they say. Actually, Anglicanism has been rather strict in matters of practice, even when it seems lax in expounding the theology behind these practices. For instance, it has insisted throughout its history on an invariable practice of episcopal ordination, and this does imply a conception of ministry, though there could be some variation when it came to formulating this in words. Again, the practice of reverently consuming the consecrated gifts at the end of the eucharist does imply some eucharistic theology, and although this too could be formulated in quite a number of ways, it is obviously a very different theology from that which prevails in those Protestant churches where any bread and wine left over is thrown in the trash-can or poured down the sink. Whether, however, practice alone is adequate to define doctrine is a question that we must raise later.

I said that Stephen Sykes' book was a timely one, for it came out just on the eve of the Lambeth Conference of 1978. That conference (like so many others) was meeting in a time of theological confusion. There was renewed controversy over christological issues. A number of ecumenical discussions in different parts of the Anglican communion had come to nothing. Matters had not been much helped by the publication in 1976 of *Christian Believing*, the report of a Doctrine Commission that had been set up by the Archbishops of Canterbury and York ten years earlier. I was myself a member of that commission from 1970 onwards, and I think I am correct in saying that I remember it as a group of individualists. Its members were accustomed to make set speeches that were often quite lengthy and rarely related to one another. There was very little in the way of genuine discussion. As was noted both in the foreword by Donald Coggan and in the preface by Maurice Wiles (who had succeeded Ian Ramsey as chairman of the commission), the brief unanimous statement which forms the principal part of the report had been arrived at only with the greatest difficulty and is mainly concerned to stress the fluidity and pluralism which characterize contemporary theology. One of the members of the commission, Geoffrey Lampe, describes its report as a 'plea for coexistence', and says that 'it suggests that unity in the future will be a unity in asking questions rather than agreeing to answers'.[7] This is not a very happy prospect, if the church thinks it has anything to say to contemporary society. There was in fact general disappointment with the report. Lampe reminds us that it was never discussed in the councils of the church, never commended to the church at large, attracted little public comment and, as he put it, was quietly and rapidly buried.[8]

Archbishop Coggan lost no time in appointing a new commission, with an almost entirely different membership, presumably in the hope of getting more positive results. The chairman this time was John Taylor, Bishop of Winchester, and *Believing in the Church* was the deliberately ambiguous title of the report which the new commission issued in 1981. A major concern of the commission was the corporate nature of faith, and how the corporate faith of the church is related to the varieties of faith found among individual members. There seems to have been some danger that questions about the truth and falsehood of doctrine might be submerged in the idea that corporate beliefs are primarily expressions of the solidarity of the community – the chairman, for instance, wrote that 'believing is mainly belonging'.[9] But the philosopher, Basil Mitchell, precisely reverses this relation and declares that 'to belong to a church is to believe what the church believes'.[10] Another member of the commission, John Bowker, a theologian who is also competent in information theory, seemed to be criticizing the sloppiness of much Anglican theology when he declared: 'Information does not just slop around the universe in a random or arbitrary manner; it is channeled and protected, coded and organized.'[11] Admittedly, doctrines are not adequately equated with 'information'. But it has always been held that they have some cognitive content, and to the extent that they do, one has to be concerned with their truth and internal consistency.

The report of 1981, therefore, more than its predecessor of five years earlier, tends to support Stephen Sykes' view that there is a definite Anglican doctrinal position. In a composite chapter written by three members of the commission, the bases of doctrine are spelled out more fully than had been done by Sykes. One of the writers describes what he calls 'doctrine declared', that is to say, doctrine made explicit in written statements. He thinks of a kind of pyramid, with the Bible at the top, then the creeds, the articles, the Prayer Book, the ordinal, the canons, pronouncements of Lambeth conferences and, presumably a step lower, of the General Synod. Perhaps a place would have to be found too for documents like those produced by ARCIC on the eucharist, ministry and authority, for although these have not as yet been officially approved by the Church of England, still less by the whole Anglican communion, they are not simply the work of private theologians but of theologians officially appointed to represent the Anglican point of view. A second section of this chapter deals with 'doctrine implicit', chiefly the doctrine that is implicit in the liturgy and in the way it is done. A final section entitled 'doctrine diffused' reminds us that the history of the English church has been so closely tied up with the general history of the English people that there is a kind of penumbra of doctrine continuing to subsist in 'folk religion', and although this may be unsophisticated and may verge on mere superstition, it may be useful for the church to be reminded of what people on the fringes *expect* church people to believe.

Stephen Sykes also called for a more serious engagement with systematic theology among Anglican theologians, and I have much sympathy myself with this view. I have said already that, properly understood, systematic theology does not freeze the issues. It always has an open and provisional character – this is true alike of Barth, Tillich and Rahner, to mention three recent practitioners – and in no way inhibits that theological freedom which is part of the Anglican heritage. The neglect of systematic theology among Anglicans is due in the main, I think, to a series of historical accidents. In the first place, the Reformation in England was much less radical than in countries which went the way of Calvinism and Lutheranism, and while we may be glad of this, since it preserved strong links with the catholic tradition, it did tend to produce a kind of theological lethargy. While in other countries which had been touched by the Reformation, it was felt incumbent to produce confessions of faith and, very soon, textbooks of dogmatics, the Church of England believed itself to have abided by the faith of the universal church. The articles of faith which it produced did not attempt a systematic statement of Christian theology as a whole, but only dealt with those matters where Anglicanism had broken with certain ideas which had prevailed in the mediaeval period. This already introduced that lack of proportion which we noted as characteristic of the 1938 report, *Doctrine in the Church of England*, where matters of ecclesiology receive far more space and attention than what one might consider the more fundamental doctrines of God, Christ and salvation. A second point is that the preoccupation with the Bible and the Fathers in Anglican theology has tended to stifle development and creativity. This is especially true since the rise of the critical historical method. As Sykes points out,[12] it has led to a type of theology which is parasitic, in the sense that it criticizes the tradition but makes no contribution of its own to what ought to be a growing, expanding tradition. To a large extent, we have to look to the continent for creative theology, for genuinely new Christian insights that seek to express the inherited truths in the thought-forms of our own time. Regrettably, one has got to admit that there is some truth in the old quip that theology is created in Europe, corrected in England and corrupted in the United States! This leaves to England the necessary but hardly exalted task of correcting the work of others. Even this task, it must be confessed, is often neglected, for Anglican theology tends to be somewhat insular, and one is often astonished in looking through the index of English theological works to note the almost complete neglect of continental theologians and philosophers who have had an influence on theology. To give an example, a collection of essays by Cambridge scholars on christology (of which, incidentally, Stephen Sykes was one of the editors),[13] made no mention at all of Rahner, in spite of his very important contributions to this subject! The only non-British theologian to get any coverage was Tillich, and that was in a chapter contributed by an American! This gives me the opportunity of saying that the final part of the quip which I quoted, about theology's being corrupted in the United States, is certainly not true today, if it ever was. American theology, just as much as European theology, has shown itself to be imaginative and constructive.

So far I have been talking about Anglican theology in general, and especially about the ways in which it has found expression in the liturgy and in various official doctrinal pronouncements of the church. I would now like to turn our attention to the long line of individual Anglican theologians who have been writing in the past four centuries or thereabouts. They form a varied company, as indeed we might expect after what we have seen of the broad limits within which Anglican theology goes on, yet we can discern a kind of family resemblance among them.

Let us go back to Cranmer, perhaps the principal architect of the Reformation in England. His major theological work, published in 1550, bears as its full title: *A Defence of the True and Catholic Doctrine of the Sacrament of the Body and Blood of our Saviour Christ: with a Confutation of Sundry Errors concerning the Same, Grounded and Stablished upon God's Holy Word, and Approved by the Consent of the most Ancient Doctors of the Church.* This very title tells us quite a lot. In the first place, it is no specifically Anglican doctrine that he intends to set forth, but 'the true and catholic doctrine'. In the second place, he intends to base himself on scripture, and secondarily on the Fathers of the Church, whose interpretation of the scriptures he hopes to show are supportive of his own. In the book itself, he enlarges his norms by including reason, claiming that in his teaching 'nothing is spoken either contrary to holy scripture, or to natural reason, philosophy or experience, or against any old ancient author, or the primitive or catholic church; but only against the malignant and papistical church of Rome'.[14] Here then already in Cranmer we have a clear statement of the essential characteristics of Anglican theology, which bases itself first on the scriptures, next on the teachings of the early church and its doctors, and finally on reason and experience.

Still in the sixteenth century, an important work was that of John Jewel, who about 1560 wrote *An Apology of the Church of England*. The most important part of this work is a defence of the Church of England against the charge of heresy. In successive sections, Jewel rehearses the beliefs of the church: 'We believe that there is one certain nature and divine power which we call God. . .' He then speaks of the three persons of the Trinity, then of the church (not omitting 'that there be diverse degrees of ministers in the church; whereof some be deacons, some priests, some bishops'), and goes on then to the sacraments, which, he says, are not 'cold ceremonies', for 'we affirm that Christ doth truly and presently give his own self in the sacraments'.[15] Jewel's apology was directed mainly to defending the Church of England against the attacks of Rome. One of Jewel's pupils was Richard Hooker, whose *Laws of Ecclesiastical Polity* appeared between thirty and forty years after Jewel's *Apology*. Hooker's defence of the church was directed more against the Puritans, and between them these two early Anglican writers clearly marked out the *via media* of the Church of England: Catholic, in that she believed herself to continue in all essentials the church of the early centuries; Reformed, in that she also thought it an obligation to rid herself of some of the doctrinal and practical innovations that had come along in the Middle Ages. But Hooker made it quite clear that the church is not frozen to the actual explicit words of scripture. Tradition and reason were assured of a place alongside scripture, though subordinate to it.

Not for nothing has the epithet 'judicious' been applied to Richard Hooker. With admirable judgment, he held together on most matters the Anglican 'troika' of scripture, tradition and reason. It was inevitable, however, that this judicious balance would be lost by lesser men. Nevertheless, in the century after Hooker, the type of theology which he had created remained dominant in Anglicanism. The seventeenth century was indeed the golden age of classical Anglicanism, the era of the Caroline divines such as Lancelot Andrewes, William Laud, Jeremy Taylor and others. According to the historian John Moorman, it was their contribution which enabled the church to rise again after the disasters of the Civil War and the Commonwealth. The attitude of this group is summed up in the last words of Bishop Thomas Ken: 'I die in the holy catholic and apostolic faith, professed by the whole church before the disunion of east and west. More particularly, I die in the communion of the Church of England as it stands distinguished from all papal and puritan innovations, and as it adheres to the doctrine of the cross.'[16] No doubt the Church of England has often been far removed from this lofty vision, yet one may claim that the ideal of the *via media*, a pure and primitive catholicism, fostered by these seventeenth-century divines, has never ceased to inspire the Anglican communion.

In the eighteenth century, the so-called Age of Reason, there was inevitably a swing toward rationalism. The extreme form of this rationalism was, of course, deism, and it was an Anglican priest, Matthew Tindal, who became one of the leaders of that school of thought. His book, with the self-explanatory title, *Christianity as Old as the Creation, or, The Gospel a Republication of the Religion of Nature* (1730), became virtually the 'Bible' of deism. The deists were opposed by Joseph Butler, perhaps the greatest of all Anglican theologians, but the effectiveness of his opposition to deism was due in no small measure to the way in which he incorporated rationalism into his own theology. At the same time evangelicalism became a force to reckon with. Its most famous representatives, Wesley and Whitefield, clashed sharply with Butler when the latter was Bishop of Bristol, and eventually they passed out of the Church of England. But a powerful evangelical influence remained, as did also a lingering residue of deism, manifesting itself from time to time in the extreme liberalism or near-unitarianism of some far out groups and individuals.

In the nineteenth century the Oxford Movement tried to recapture the spirit of classical Anglicanism. Keble himself edited a new edition of the works of Richard Hooker. Newman wrote eloquently of the *via media* and declared about the formularies of the Church of England: 'It is a duty which we owe both to the catholic church and to ourselves to take our reformed confessions in the most catholic sense they will admit.'[17] It was surely a great tragedy for the Church of England and for Anglican theology that he later turned away from his early convictions. Pusey too was reviving the traditional Anglican way of theologizing. When a sermon of his on the eucharist was condemned by the university authorities at Oxford, he proceeded to show that his teachings about the real presence and the eucharistic sacrifice were all derived from ancient Christian authorities, in case, as he said, his judges through ignorance might find themselves condemning 'St Cyril of Alexandria, when they thought they were only condemning me'.[18]

There can be no doubt that the Oxford Movement did much towards reviving in the Church of England an appreciation of the distinctive Anglican theological tradition, and this has been apparent both in official pronouncements of the church since the time of the Movement and in the work of many individual theologians. But even in the nineteenth century, it was already too late to restore the synthesis of the classical divines of the sixteenth and seventeenth centuries, even if that had been thought desirable. Anglicanism, like other Christian communions, including even that of Rome, has entered on a time of theological pluralism. Perhaps the most we can hope is that the authentic spirit of the *via media* will continue as a strong influence among the conflicting movements of the present time, insuring the continuance of a Christian theology rooted in the biblical witness, true to the catholic tradition and commending itself by its inherent truth to reasonable men and women.

10

Pride in the Church

Some years ago there appeared in *The Times*[1] an article
entitled 'Recovering the Mystery of the Right Kind of
Triumphalism'. I suppose many another reader besides
myself must have rubbed his eyes and looked again. How
could there be a 'right kind' of triumphalism? Surely
triumphalism, as we have been hearing at least since the
days of Vatican II, is pride in the church, and that is wrong.
In the triumphalist era the church attempted to lord it over
the world, whereas her true role is now said to be to serve
the needs of the world.

Next I noted that the article was not, as one might have
expected, the work of some diehard ultramontanist from the
Curia, unable to reconcile himself with the changes that
have taken place in the Roman Catholic Church. In fact it
appeared over the name of an Anglican churchman, Mervyn
Stockwood, formerly Bishop of Southwark. His diocese had
for many years been noted as the home of the ongoings of
'South Bank religion' and was accounted perhaps the most
radical (though certainly not the most successful) in England.
The first paragraph explained that the bishop had derived
his inspiration from some remarks made by a prominent
Protestant churchman, the leader of the Taizé community.
He had recently been suggesting that anti-triumphalism has
been carried to such extremes that matters of real importance
and value, especially in liturgy and worship, are in danger
of being lost or severely damaged. We are nowadays familiar
with situations in which Anglican or Protestant churchmen
take it upon themselves to defend elements of the catholic
heritage that are being threatened by the zeal of Roman

reformers, and this is understandable. The role of Protestantism within the total fabric of Christianity is essentially a critical and reforming one. Paul Tillich aptly described the relation as the application of the Protestant principle to the Catholic substance. But where the solidity of the Catholic substance is itself in danger of dissolution, the Protestant principle becomes otiose.

I shall return eventually to this problem of triumphalism and anti-triumphalism, and whether there could be a 'right kind' of triumphalism as the Bishop of Southwark and the Prior of Taizé claimed. But if triumphalism is properly described as 'pride in the church', then the question of triumphalism must be preceded by a brief consideration of pride. If there is a right kind of triumphalism, this must be a right kind of pride in the church. Perhaps there is no right kind of pride in the church, but even at the outset of our consideration we can see that the expression 'pride in the church' is an ambiguous one and that it might not be equally objectionable in all its senses. 'Pride in the church' might mean the presence of pride among those who constitute the church, or at least among some of them. It might take the form of a prelatical mentality among the leaders or a pharisaical self-righteousness among the ordinary members or a feeling of superiority among Christians with regard to adherents of other faiths. These forms of pride would all be deplorable. But 'pride in the church' could also mean taking pride in its past history or its present activities, or at least some of these, and it is not immediately obvious that this kind of pride is as deplorable as the other.

Unquestionably Christian moral theology has consistently regarded pride as sinful. It was counted one of the seven deadly sins, and has often been thought to be the most deadly of all, the primordial sin from which all the others have been derived. Augustine, for instance, traces back even the sins of the flesh to pride. 'If anyone says,' he writes, 'that the flesh is the cause of all vices and ill conduct, it is certain that he has not carefully considered the whole nature of man. . . Of all these evils, pride is the origin, and it rules in the devil, though he has no flesh.'[2] In modern theology,

Reinhold Niebuhr has been the great castigator of the sin of pride. At one period of his writing, the Tower of Babel was his favourite symbol, and when we recall that he was working during the time of the rise of the Nazi state, we can well understand his mistrust of pride and of every glorification of the human institution. One of Niebuhr's insights, to which we shall find ourselves returning later, was that there is no monopoly of pride, whether in secular or religious matters. On the specific question of pride in the church, he claimed (but let us remember that this was twenty years before Vatican II) that the Roman Catholic Church had made too simple an identification of the human institution with the Kingdom of God. 'This identification,' he wrote, 'which allows a religious institution involved in all the relativities of history to claim unconditioned truth for its doctrines and unconditioned moral authority for its standards, makes it just another tool of human pride.' But to this Protestant criticism, he went on with admirable fairness to add: 'As soon as the Protestant assumes that his more prophetic stance and interpretation of the Christian gospel guarantee him a superior virtue, he is also lost in the sin of self-righteousness.'[3]

Nevertheless, while pride might qualify as the primordial sin and while the ravages of the will to power have been terrible indeed in human history, there are surely forms of pride which are scarcely blameworthy. The momentary flush of pride which an athlete feels when, by a supreme effort, he has broken a record seems natural and right. Even more so is the pride which others may feel in his achievement. Such pride becomes sinful and blameworthy only when it settles into a hardened attitude of superiority or when it becomes egocentric and issues in an exclusive and contemptuous attitude toward others. Alas! this is often what happens in religion.

But perhaps in the Christian tradition the contrast between pride and humility has been drawn too starkly. If we consider the synonyms and near-synonyms for 'pride', such as 'haughtiness', 'conceit', 'vanity', 'insolence', 'self-esteem', and the like, what we seem to have is a spectrum of attitudes, reaching on the one side towards a thoroughly blameworthy arrogance but on the other towards independence and a realistic judgment of worth. We may then have to modify the contrast between the sin of an overweening arrogance and the Christian ideal of perfect meekness by recognizing that there are many nuances. Indeed, in our ordinary situations, one rarely meets the extremes, and most of the time we are encountering intermediate attitudes, some good and some bad.

We can better understand the complexities if we attend to what Aristotle had to say about pride. He sees proper pride as a mean between two extremes. At the one extreme is vanity. The vain man is 'he who thinks himself worthy of great things, being unworthy of them'. At the other extreme is undue humility. 'The man who thinks of himself less than he is really worthy of, is unduly humble.' Pride is intermediate. 'The man is thought to be proud who thinks himself worthy of great things, being worthy of them.'[4] Admittedly, Aristotle's proud man may not strike us as a very attractive character, but his analysis is important as showing that there are forms of pride which are not altogether blameworthy and likewise that there are forms of humility which may not be praiseworthy.

Still further subtleties are introduced by some modern philosophical and psychological analyses of dominance and submission. I have in mind, for instance, Hegel's famous exploration of the master-slave relation[5] and Sartre's closely parallel description of sadism and masochism in the sexual relation.[6] What these writers reveal is the way in which the opposites tend to pass over into each other. The proud dominance of the master and the possessiveness of the sadist are alike haunted by insecurity and result in a dependence on the other person in the relationship. On the other side, submissiveness and masochism may mask a desire for power. No doubt moral judgments are still possible, and one may judge the master to be more blameworthy than the slave and the sadist than the masochist. But these judgments have become relative, and no one is totally acquitted of pride and the desire for domination. Even such an apparently clearcut case as that of the Pharisee and the taxman praying in the temple is not entirely without its ambiguities. Certainly the story comes down heavily against those 'who trusted in themselves that they were righteous and despised others' (Luke 18.9). But it is possible to boast of one's sins as well as of one's righteousness, and it may be doubted whether there is any humility that is entirely free from a taint of self-justifying pride. In this parable, one man is justified rather than the other, and clearly he is justified a long way ahead of the other. But this is still a relative judgment. It is not said that one man is completely justified and the other totally condemned, for no person or group ever has a monopoly of sin in human society.

Perhaps we have sufficiently explored the general concept of pride to be able to come back now to the special problem of triumphalism or pride in the church, and in particular to the question whether there could be a right kind of triumphalism.

There are probably very few people today, even among the most reactionary, who would wish to defend the older triumphalism. We must remember, of course, that such triumphalism never wholly permeated the church and that at any given time there were plenty of good Christians, both Catholic and Protestant, both clerical and lay, whose faith and way of life were simple and unassuming. But there were bishops and clergy who lived ostentatiously, and it was generally accepted that they should do so. There was the intellectual arrogance which prompted such unhappy events as the issuing of the *Syllabus Errorum* in condemnation of modern thought, or the hasty ridiculing by Anglican divines of the theory of evolution. There was pride in ecclesiastical office and an eagerness for preferment scarcely appropriate in those who counted themselves ministers or servants of Jesus Christ. There was (and several chapters of this book protest against it) the dismissive attitudes on the part of Christians towards other faiths, even the Jewish faith, which Kant, Schleiermacher and many other distinguished scholars declared to have no connection with Christianity – a point which long after was cited by the Nazis in defence of their anti-Semitic policies. Many, though not all, of these evil forms of triumphalism have gone, and no one would wish to see them return.

But what do we have now in place of the old triumphalism? I think there are several new stances that have taken its place, and some of them seem almost as unsatisfactory.

Some in the church, including some bishops and clergy, have gone to the opposite exteme and we observe among them what Aristotle called 'undue humility'. Nowadays we might regard it as a kind of masochism. They have become so afraid of seeming to dominate either society at large or their fellow churchmen and have so muted their voices that they provide no real leadership and cause people generally to suppose that the Christian church is now utterly bewildered and has lost its nerve and its sense of purpose. The sociologist Peter Berger expressed this very pungently in relation to the churches of the United States: 'Mainline Protestantism is marked by a widespread demoralization that has quite properly been called a general failure of nerve. Its expressions range from masochistic self-laceration to hysterical defensiveness, but hardly anyone has remained untouched by it. If it has been suggested rather nastily that the institutional efforts to cope with the crisis are like rearranging the deck-chairs on the *Titanic*, then it may be added that some of the critics of the institution have in effect been saying that we should blow up the ship before it even gets to the iceberg. Also, we are in good company now. The Catholics who, back in 1961, still seemed to be sitting pretty on their Rock of Peter, are now looking for trustworthy lifeboats like the rest of us.'[7]

Pride and humility, sadism and masochism, dominance and servility are strangely mingled in the church as elsewhere, and if some seem to have lost their nerve in undue humility, pride has found a home elsewhere. If pride is a hardening of the sense of superiority, a secure self-righteousness that cannot bear criticism or hear another point of view, an exclusive contempt for those who are different, then one must acknowledge that there is still pride in the church today, but surprisingly it seems to have found its stronghold precisely among the anti-triumphalists, the so-called radicals who know precisely what the church is and what it ought to be doing and who have no time for anything that does not fit into their programme. I doubt if there could be any greater arrogance than is to be found among those Christians who speak as if they are the first people in two thousand years of history really to understand what Christianity is all about.

It is often said nowadays that the church is as deeply divided as ever it was, no longer along denominational lines but along new lines which cut across the old ones. We frequently hear the word 'polarization' referring to the hardening of attitudes, and that hardening and the pride which leads to it are by no means confined to any one group. Pride and its infinite variations, combinations and permutations still work in the church and still work havoc in the church. Is there any way in which we can be delivered?

There is a possible deliverance. The pride which hardens persons and leads them to be deaf to one another and even to despise one another can be overcome if both sides are brought into a presence which humbles them both. And there is only one presence where that can happen – the presence of God. Pride itself is a kind of idolatry and it is possible only in the absence of God. We make our own opinions ultimate and perhaps even claim that they are what God wants, and in some measure this happens to all of us, whether we call ourselves conservative or liberal or radical or whether we even take pride in not having a label. This kind of idolatrous pride, whether it divides the church within itself or from those outside, is destructive. But the cure for it is to take a higher view of the church. The church is not, as Niebuhr reminded us, the Kingdom of God; but neither is the church a merely human institution that must forever yield to human pride and passions. The church shows, even if only weakly and fitfully, a hidden glory that is striving to find expression and realization. The church is not the Kingdom of God, but it is the people of God, a part of humanity where God is seeking to manifest his purpose for the whole human race.

At this point we come back to the question raised by Mervyn Stockwood about a right kind of triumphalism. This right kind of triumphalism is the exaltation of God in his church, especially in worship. Much of the liturgical innovation of recent years has been drab, utilitarian and uninspiring. Worship should, among other things, be impressing upon us the glory and splendour of God which should be coming to manifestation in the church. Where God is truly exalted in the church, the pride of factions and individuals is curbed. We recognize that the church is not our creation to be moulded according to our ideas, but is the people of God, a people on its way towards God, though still far short of his Kingdom. And this in turn curbs any proud feelings towards those who are seeking God by a different route. All humanity is potentially the people of God and the concern of God. This means that the Christian should not have feelings of pride or superiority, even though fully committed to his faith. Are not the Jews too the people of God? Are not the outcastes of India, whom some called 'untouchables', also known as '*harijan*', 'people of the Lord'? Christians must repent of every proud word and act by which they have arrogated God's glory to themselves and have spurned either fellow Christians or men and women of other faiths, but this must not prevent them from recognizing that in spite of human sinfulness there are manifestations of the divine glory in the church and that it is right for them to give it their wholehearted loyalty.

11

The Idea of a People of God

One of the most typical ideas in the Judaeo-Christian tradition is that of a people of God. The idea is equally important in both the Jewish and Christian branches of the tradition. Israel is the elect of God, the people he has formed for himself; they will be his people and he will be their God (Isa. 42.1; 62.12; etc). Likewise, the Christian church has believed itself to be a chosen generation, a royal priesthood, a holy nation, a peculiar people (1 Peter 2.9).

Is this idea of a people of God, as many have complained, a restrictive, separatist, élitist idea? Does it lead to an exclusiveness and sense of superiority on the part of those who think of themselves as belonging to the elect people? It has sometimes been alleged that the Judaeo-Christian tradition has been more intolerant than, let us say, some of the East Asian religious traditions. It may indeed be the case that the idea of a people of God has sometimes been interpreted along exclusivist lines, but this need not be the case, and it has not been the case in those moments of deepest insight among those who have thought of themselves as the people of God. The very use of the word people in the expression people of God is highly significant. It shows we have to do with *people*, with a human reality, and because of this, the expression relates somehow to all people, to humanity as such. In what it had to say about the church, Vatican II made the idea of a people of God fundamental. Because of this, it was able to present a far more open view of the church than was possible when the understanding of the church was presented under more restrictive images, such as 'the Body of Christ' or, even more, the ark of salvation floating upon the stormy waters. These two images, especially the second of them, tended to stress the discontinuity of the church with the world around, whereas the image of the people of God tends to stress continuity with the whole human race, even with people of other faiths.

It is not only the word 'people' in the expression 'people of God' that broadens the reference, for the broadening is carried even further by the use of the word 'God'. A universal reference is hidden in this word, for God is believed to be the author and ruler of all. One of the most central teachings in the Judaeo-Christian tradition is the doctrine of creation. According to this teaching, the whole universe, including the entire human race, are creatures of God, and this can only mean that, at least ideally, the entire human race is the people of God.

Let us consider a little more closely this expression, 'the people of God'. Superficially, it apears to be a descriptive phrase, similar, let us say, to 'the people of Mexico', 'the people of the Stone Age', 'the people of the Amazon basin', or whatever it might be. But the resemblance is only superficial, for when we say, 'the people *of God*', we introduce a new dimension of meaning which sets this phrase apart from the examples quoted, 'the people of Mexico', 'the people of the Stone Age', and the like. The latter are simply factual descriptions of groups of human beings, distinguished by the circumstance that they share a common citizenship or lived during a particular epoch or are found in a certain geographical area, but the expression 'people of God' neither can nor does function in any such way. 'The people of God' is a typical piece of religious language. It takes a word with ordinary empirical reference, in this case the word 'people', meaning a group of human beings, perhaps a nation or some other more or less clearly defined segment or community. The religious phrase then does refer to something within our ordinary range of experience, people who can be seen and heard, loved or hated, admired or despised, people who have a share in shaping the history of our planet. But where it differs from any ordinary description is in its use of the words, 'of God'. This people is not defined by any empirical

characteristics, such as citizenship, language, ethnic inheritance, cultural peculiarities, or anything of the sort. Any or
all of these may, of course, be present in varying degrees, but
they are not *defining* characteristics. This people is defined as
being 'of God' – elect of God, belonging to God, summoned
by God, sanctified of God, even, it may be, alienated from
God, but always defined by the relation to God. But God is
not an empirical phenomenon within the world. The
expression, 'the people of God', is what I have called 'a
typical piece of religious language' because it takes an
empirical concept, namely, people, and then by qualifying
this through relating it to the key word of all religion, trans-
forms it into a transempirical concept. This people is to be
seen in a new dimension of depth, in a new set of relations
which lie beyond those discoverable by empirical observation. To explore further what this means will be one of
our main tasks in this chapter.

A good starting point for this exploration is the cycle of
stories in *Genesis* relating to Abraham. He is often called 'the
first man of faith', though from the very beginning Abraham
appears as not just an individual but as the leader and
representative of a community. The ancient stories of Abraham's journeys and adventures do not, of course, introduce
explicitly those modern sophisticated philosophical problems
on which I have just touched – problems about the use of
language, the theory of descriptions, the question of
empirical verification and the like – but they do show an
astonishing insight into the nature and destiny of the human
race as it strives to become a people worthy of the name of
people, a true people of God. In that cycle of Abraham
stories there is already contained *in nuce* most of the fundamental themes that were to be unfolded in the subsequent
development of the Judaeo-Christian tradition, and, not least
among them, the theme of a people of God.

The first story in the Abraham saga tells of his departure
from the city of Haran in Mesopotamia. The history of the
people of God begins with an act of separation, and something like this is necessary in order to establish an identity.
No doubt Abraham had been successful enough in Haran –

he seems to have been already a man of substance. But he found no true contentment in that affluent society. He was ready to move on to something else, and something better, even if he did not quite know what it would be. He was ready, we could say, for the voice of God and the summons to a new life. We are told that he heard the divine voice commanding him: 'Get thee out of thy country, and from thy kindred, and from thy father's house, unto a land that I will show thee.' But it was not just a command that the voice spoke, it was also a promise: 'I will make of thee a great nation, and I will bless thee, and make thy name great; and thou shalt be a blessing . . . and in thee shall all families of the earth be blessed' (Gen. 12.1–2). These few verses are laden with profound meaning. The people of God has been from the beginning a dynamic people, a people on the move. It cannot settle down where it is, it must move on, both driven by a divine discontent and drawn by a divine promise. This indeed implies separation from and departure out of the environing society – the people of God could never have been born if Abraham and his companions had been content to stay part of Mesopotamian society, had continued to accept its standards and follow its customs, and had never looked beyond its mode of life. Abraham turned his back on that settled society and headed into the wilderness of the south – the wilderness where the land was still virgin and had not yet been given shape, and where a new society could be built on principles different from those which governed the old. It is a picture that ought to have a special appeal to Americans, as they remember how the forefathers of their nation turned their backs on Europe to risk everything for the sake of building a new society in a virgin land. The separation was necessary, but it must have been painful, and we must note that from the beginning the separation was never conceived as a sheer abandonment. The promise was that through Abraham all the families of the earth would find blessing, and this would include the families that he had left behind in Haran.

The people of God exists in a dialectical relation to the human race at large. To become the people of God, it must take upon itself a distinctive existence, and this is necessary if it is to serve any purpose at all. Yet, it remains linked at a deep level to the human race as a whole and will eventually prove a blessing to all.

We could go further, and say that this story about the beginning of the people of God is a parable of the situation of the whole human race. The entire race is on a pilgrimage into the wilderness of the unknown. The entire race is in search of a true humanity and a true community. The entire race is summoned to set out from where it is at any given time in quest of something new and better. The entire race is stirred by divine discontent and drawn by divine promise, even if these are often suppressed and forgotten. For it is all too easy for human beings to settle down where they are, to evade the labours and anxieties of pilgrimage, to be content with the familiar and to seek to establish what is intended to be an enduring, unchanging order. That is why a special people of God is needed – a minority who will not stay put but will insist on going on to something new and better, yet not for themselves alone but for the ultimate blessing of all.

The very next story in the Abraham saga (Gen. 12.14–20) is a sharp rebuke to any who might suppose that the people of God is a superior élite, impervious to the sins and temptations of ordinary mortals. There was a famine, and Abraham went down to Egypt in search of sustenance. But he was very anxious about what might happen to him there. In particular, he knew that his wife Sarah was a woman of great beauty, and he was afraid that some Egyptian potentate might have him killed in order to take possession of his wife. So he practised a deception. He pretended that Sarah was his sister, and let her be taken into the harem of the king of Egypt, while he himself received generous gifts from the king in return for the favour he had shown him. Even in those ancient times (or, should I say, especially in those ancient times?), Abraham's action was regarded as mean, sordid and shameful. But the story was not suppressed when Israel's historians came to write up the chronicles of the people. It was allowed to stand in the record, near the beginning of the whole epic of God's people. It is a perpetual reminder that there is neither instant perfection nor automatic progress in the life of the people of God – indeed, the very possibility of progress means that there must also be the possibility of regress, and, as a matter of historical fact, the people of God, whether in its Jewish or its Christian manifestation, has had many backslidings. Not seldom, its leaders have manifested less integrity that pagans and secularists, just as did Abraham in his dealings with the king of Egypt.

There is another remarkable story which speaks very plainly of the continuing solidarity between the people of God and the rest of the human race (Gen. 18.16–23). Indeed, it expresses in story form something which remains a mystery even for our most sophisticated philosophies of human nature, namely, that there are hidden but nonetheless powerful ties that bind all mankind in a single bundle of life. Abraham's companion, Lot, who had been one of the company that departed from Haran and therefore himself one of the people of God, had separated himself from Abraham. He had perhaps found the demands of the new life more than he had expected and longed for the urban comforts that he had known in Haran. So he had chosen for himself and his flocks the most fertile part of the land in the vicinity of the cities of Sodom and Gomorrah, while Abraham sojourned in the wilderness country towards the south. It would not be unfair to say that Lot had lapsed back into the old life, that he had become an apostate and had fallen away from his vocation to the people of God. Abraham himself could have had no sympathy with him. Indeed, Lot's action was threatening the very existence of the new community as it struggled for survival. Abraham must have had even less sympathy with Lot's new associates, the people of Sodom and Gomorrah. These cities represented the very worst of the kind of life that Abraham was trying to leave behind. They were a byword for the life of luxury, self-indulgence, materialism, hedonism, vice. Yet when Lot was taken prisoner by some invading armies, it was Abraham who went to his rescue. What is even more remarkable, when the Lord was determined to destroy the cities of the plain for their wickedness, it was Abraham who interceded for them. There are few more poignant passages in the Bible than Abraham's pleading before God for Sodom and Gomorrah – if there are fifty righteous people in these cities, spare them; if there are forty-five, forty, thirty, twenty, ten . . . What is the meaning of this prayer? It certainly gives the lie to any accusation that the elect people had turned its back on mankind, and was concerned only for itself. What we have here is the remarkable dialectic of separation and solidarity, characteristic of the people's life. There had to be separation. The chosen people had to distance itself, sometimes in prophetic denunciation, from whatever mars and destroys the truly human quality of life. But deeper than the separation is the solidarity, the kinship with all fellow human beings, who are also potentially the people of God even if they have turned away from their true destiny and there is hardly a trace of righteousness to be found among them.

We cannot explore all the Abraham stories, instructive though they are, but there is one more than cannot be ignored, for it is both the best known and the most difficult of all – the story of how the divine voice commands Abraham to sacrifice his only son, Isaac, and of how Abraham demonstrates his willingness to obey even this terrible command (Gen. 22.1–14). In a famous discussion of this incident, Søren Kierkegaard claimed that there are moments in life when a higher obligation demands that we set aside the ordinary claims of morality and of natural affection in order to obey the higher claim.[1] It may be questioned whether Kierkegaard was quite successful in his attempt to interpret the story, though it has also to be remembered that at the end of the day the sacrifice of Isaac was not required, and that God himself provided a sacrifice in Isaac's place. But whatever argument there might be over interpreting the details of this story, some points seem to be clear enough. The way of the people of God will be a costly way, of struggle and suffering and sacrifice. It will not be a way of privilege and triumph. Yet there is also the assurance that the people are not alone in their suffering and sacrifice – God is with them, he even shares their suffering and provides their sacrifices. One is reminded of a recurring phrase in Abraham Heschel's writings about Israel – 'the *pathos* of God'.[2]

How these thoughts were developed in the prophetic tradition of Israel is well known. That tradition culminates in the idea of the suffering servant, despised and rejected by men, yet charged with a mission to the nations and upheld by God. (Isa. 42.1–4 and 53). And this prophetic vision was no mere idea, but has been concrete in the actual historical sufferings of Israel, not only those recorded in the Bible but those that have followed down to the present day. And who can doubt that these have also been the sufferings and sacrifices of God? In the words of a late prophet, 'In all their afflictions, he was afflicted' (Isa. 63.9).

As I mentioned, all the essential characteristics of the people of God are already presented in symbolic or narrative form in the Abraham cycle of stories. These characteristics all reappear in the Christian church, which has also claimed to be a people of God, and which, in its being and history, has shown many remarkable parallels with Israel. There has been the same dialectic of separation and solidarity. The church could only come into being by asserting its distinctiveness from Israel. For the first three centuries of its existence it lived on the margin of society, cut off from the mainstream of life in the Roman Empire, a suspect and often persecuted sect. Yet even at that time, within the church, there was taking place a remarkable breaking down of barriers between social and ethnic groups, and there was emerging a new sense of human solidarity. Again, like Israel before it, the church had many backslidings, and there have been many occasions when she was tempted by the triumphalism of power, forgetting that all human existence is pilgrimage and that the goal of a truly mature people of God has not yet been attained. There have been times of arrogance when the church has sought to dominate the world, forgetting the New Testament teaching that it is meant to be the leaven that leavens the whole lump, not the lump itself (Luke 13.21). The church too has shrunk from the costliness and sacrifice which are demanded from the people of God, though in its finest hours it has remembered that its symbol is the cross, and that its greatest achievements have been purchased with the blood of its martyrs and saints. The church, after all, is the church of Jesus Christ, indeed, it claims to be his Body, an extension into subsequent history of his life of love and service. But Jesus Christ was not only the founder of the Christian community, he was also a true son of Israel, and it was a true insight that led some of his earliest followers to connect him with the suffering servant of the Lord portrayed in Deutero-Isaiah. That suffering servant is at one and the same time the people of Israel, Jesus Christ, and the Christian church – they are all manifestations of the life that is defined by the relation to God.

But how can I say such a thing – that the Jewish people and the Christian church are both manifestations of the people of God? Is this not to ignore far too blandly the tragic history of the relations between Jews and Christians – relations which, from the very beginning, have been marked not so much by friendship or awareness of a common mission, as by enmities, disputes, accusations, even persecutions and overt violence? One must confess that it has been a sad history. Perhaps Christians must especially confess this, since Christians have so often been in the majority and have been the instigators of persecution. Yet in such matters no group has ever a monopoly of sin. The separation in the earliest period of the new Christian sect from its Jewish matrix was the necessary consequence of the dialectical existence of a people of God. The tragedy was that only one side of the dialectic was allowed to come into play, separation, while the other side, solidarity, disappeared from view. Perhaps Paul, himself schooled in the best traditions of Judaism, had a vision of the eventual reconciliation of Jews and Christians (Rom.10 and 11), but this was not taken up by his fellow Christians.

We must hope that today we are standing at the beginning of a new era in Jewish-Christian relations. I believe that, from a theological point of view, a deeper exploration by both traditions of the idea of a people of God could go far towards bringing them closer together. Surely, both the needs of mankind and the purposes of God are big enough to make room for both peoples of God, or, should I say, for the two manifestations of the one people, existing not in competition but in complementarity.

Another serious question for both groups, Jews and Christians, is how they have related, as people of God, to other human groups that do not stand in the Judaeo-Christian tradition. To make this question quite specific, let us consider for a few moments the difficult question of the relation to Islam, for Muslims constitute the religious community that stands nearest to Jews and Christians. The religion of Islam looks back to Abraham, just as do Judaism and Christianity. Once again, however, we find that the relations among these three great religions have been far from friendly. The victorious armies of Islam, spilling out of the Arabian peninsula, overran the Christian provinces of North Africa and the Near East, and for a long time they threatened to conquer Europe itself by a two-pronged invasion through Spain in the west and the Balkans in the east. Christian Europe's reply was to hit back at Islam in the long frustrating series of expeditions which we call the Crusades. In recent years relations between Judaism and Islam have been particularly strained, and we seem to be still far removed from a solution. Yet, if Islam too looks back to Abraham, then, with all mankind, it shares in the promise that in Abraham all the families of the earth would be blessed. In fact, the promise is more specific even than that. While the main line of the people of God has descended from Abraham through Isaac, there was another line stemming from Ishmael, also a son of Abraham and traditionally regarded as the ancestor of those Semitic peoples whom today we call the Arabs. In that same cycle of stories about Abraham from which we have drawn so much, we find God reported as saying to Hagar, the bondwoman, concerning Ishmael, the son she had had by Abraham, 'I will make him a great nation'. (Gen. 21.18). So Ishmael's descendants too are a kind of people of God, and certainly they belong, as do also Hindus, Buddhists and many others, to that ideal people of God which potentially embraces the whole race. Christians and Jews are not privileged in having been called to be people of God. They have rather been given a special and sometimes heavy responsibility. They have been entrusted with a vision the origins of which go away back into biblical history. In spite of suffering and discouragement, they must go on seeking the realization of that vision, until all the peoples of the earth are embraced within it in a true peace or wholeness.

We noted that the expression 'people of God' has as its two main terms the words 'people' and 'God'. We have been thinking principally of the first of these and considering the role of a people of God as an agent of peace and reconciliation among the nations of the earth. But now we must turn to the other term, 'God'. It was this word, I said, that gives a new depth to the ordinary sense of the word 'people', that transfers it from the area of everyday discourse into that of religious language. What is the meaning of this talk of God, and what is the place of God in the life of the people? In a secularized age like ours, does it make sense to talk of God or to assign importance to him?

In order to know what the word 'God' means, or, perhaps better, to know who God is, we have to glance once more over the history of the people of God and learn how he has functioned in that history. It began with Abraham's hearing an inner voice, feeling an inner constraint or obligation, experiencing a divine discontent. He could not rest with himself as he was or with society as it was – he felt himself called out of that, even driven out of it. Not what is, but what ought to be, became important for him. That deep sense of oughtness or obligation, the drive to go beyond the facts of the empirical situation toward the realization of an as yet distant vision, is quite fundamental to the Judaeo-Christian experience of God. But the inner voice was not only command and constraint, it was also promise and hope. In a world where moral obligation has the ultimacy that the Judaeo-Christian tradition has ascribed to it, there must be moral government and therefore hope for the future. Such a world-view is theistic, and God is seen as the source and centre of all. God, conceived in this way, is well described

in the words of Matthew Arnold as 'the Power not ourselves
making for righteousness'.[3] It is this righteous Power operating in history that has again and again impressed itself on
Jew and Christian alike, especially in those great events that
they have taken as 'revelations' – so much so that they
have believed that the vast universe itself has been created,
sustained and governed by such a righteous Power. Yet this
is not some distant Power remote in the heavens, unaffected
by the sufferings of his creatures. God is close to his creation,
the fellow sufferer who is afflicted in the afflictions of his
people, the crucified God who from the beginning has been
pouring out his being in sacrificial love. The Judaeo-Christian
God is by no means an outmoded concept. Rather, this form
of theism makes more sense than any other world-view that
is current today.

Not only does it make more sense, it supplies a dynamic
of faith and hope which is not only for Jews and Christians
but for the whole human race. There is a blessing here for
all the families of earth. All humanity is seen potentially as
a people of God, brought to maturity in peace and righteousness. In spite of all their failures and backslidings, those
representative peoples, Israel and the church, have laboured
and will continue to labour for the fulfilling of the wider
vision.

12

The Meeting of Religions in the Modern World: Opportunities and Dangers

For thousands of years the several cultures of mankind and the religions belonging to them went their ways in relative isolation. To be sure, there was always some coming and going, and we are constantly surprised to discover how even in the most remote times of antiquity the migrations of peoples and the adventurous voyages of traders led to the dissemination of ideas far beyond their native regions. But in general it would be true to say that mankind was divided into fairly homogeneous cultural and religious blocks, each concentrated in a particular region of the earth's surface. Some historians have been so impressed with these divisions that they have maintained that (at least, until very recently) there has been no unitary world history but rather a collection of histories, each of them self-contained and carrying within itself the springs of its own development, flowering and eventual decline. A notable advocate of this point of view was Oswald Spengler, and it is interesting to note how he regards each culture as determined in all its aspects by certain basic world-conceptions that are essentially religious in character. More recently, Arnold Toynbee has also argued the case for viewing the past of mankind as a plurality of histories, each relatively independent. His scheme is even more elaborate than Spengler's, and recognizes more than a score of cultures or civilizations.

Both Spengler and Toynbee were forced to acknowledge

that there is some osmosis among the compartments which they had set up, and religion is seen as the medium which relates the different cultures. Spengler recognizes the role of Christianity in both Western culture and the Magian culture of the Near East, though he does indeed claim that the differences between Western and Eastern Christianity are so profound as to constitute them quite distinct religions. Toynbee entertains the possibility that Minoan religion spilled over into classical culture, where it survived in the mystery cults; and, more generally, he believes that a religion is not inexorably tied to the fate of the culture in which it has arisen. Thus one must not exaggerate the past isolation of cultures and religions. Two of the greatest religions of the world have in fact almost disappeared in their original cultural settings and have established themselves in what were once for them alien cultures. Buddhism virtually died out in India, but took roots and flourished in China, Japan Ceylon and South-East Asia; admittedly, it underwent such major transformations as to become almost two religions, the tendentiously named Mahayana and Hinayana. Christianity began as a Jewish sect but its future lay with the Gentile peoples; though here again the transformations were so great that one can recognize some force in Spengler's claim that Christianity has become two religions, the world-affirming Christianity of the West and the world-negating Christianity of the East.

The spread of Christianity and Buddhism into remote cultural regions was due to missionary effort, but one can also find in the past instances of religions influencing one another apart altogether from any missionary activity. The European Renaissance was accompanied by a great renewal of interest in Graeco-Roman philosophy, especially Stoicism, and this unquestionably affected not only the general culture of Europe at that time but the expression given to Christianity. At the time of the Enlightenment there was a cult of everything Chinese, and the residual Christianity of the West, which had assumed the form of a rationalistic deism, found its pure prototype in the religion of Confucius, where practical wisdom is unencumbered by anything beyond a bare minimum of theology and is unembarrassed by any 'primitive' appeal to numinous experience.

These contacts and reciprocal influences of earlier times are worth recalling if only to remind us that there never was a complete isolation of religions. Nevertheless, the general structure of separate religious and cultural blocs remained, until very recently indeed. The earlier contacts cannot be compared to what is happening now. For the first time, we do have a unitary world history. Not the missionary efforts of religions or the intellectual influences of philosophies have brought this about, but something quite impersonal – the impact of modern technology. From the West, it has reached out into all the world. No tribe of human beings, however remote in the forests of Brazil or the uplands of New Guinea, can escape being drawn into the common stream of the new unitary history or can opt out of the planning which envisages the total planet Earth. Peoples, languages, dress, eating habits – yes, even religions – are being intermingled all the world over. Planet Earth has become, in the often quoted expression of Marshall McLuhan, a large village. Instant communication and vastly increased mobility have thrown us all together in a way that could never have been even visualized in former times. Yet this unity, which has, so to speak, simply happened to us, is an external one and belongs only to the surface of life. We are very far from a unity of hearts and minds. In some ways, unfortunately, the external unity brought about by the fact that all human life is now being lived within a global technological framework is provoking disunity at deeper levels, for Western technology seems to be inseparable from an acquisitive mentality, even a spirit of concupiscence, and since the planet's resources for satisfying the ever rising level of demand are limited, acquisitiveness leads to competition and then to aggression. There exists in fact a technology-acquisitiveness-aggression syndrome, and no one has yet found out how to break it. We hear much about using technology for the benefit of mankind as if it were in itself quite neutral and could be turned either to good or bad uses. But this fails to probe the question of what technology is already doing to the spirit of man, to his systems of values and beliefs, to interpersonal relations, to the capacity for contemplation and adoration. The Marxist philosopher Herbert Marcuse writes: 'Technology is not neutral. The technological society is a system of domination which operates already in the concept and construction of techniques.'[1]

Of course, no one nowadays can afford to be anti-technological. The very survival of the vast numbers of people now living on the planet depends upon the smooth functioning of the gigantic technological apparatus that we have brought into existence. We can no longer do without it. But what is important is to recognize the ambiguity of what we have created. Far too many people are filled with an uncritical or even superstitious admiration for technology and its achievements. To be sure, the environmental crisis has given pause to the demand for unrestricted economic growth. We are far more aware today of the complexities of the situation than we were a generation ago. These complexities are of many kinds, and involve weighing different interests and different values against each other. Not least, they involve moral issues, especially those concerned with the more equal distribution of wealth. Such issues take us into a sphere where questions cannot be settled by techniques. But these questions too are global in their scope. Thus the fact that technology has imposed upon all of us an external framework of unity is demanding that we develop to match it and to deepen it a unity that is personal, social, moral, spiritual. Sometimes the issue is expressed in terms of a contrast between the standard of living and the quality of life. But these two are not simply to be contrasted. They are linked in subtle ways that include elements both of contrast and affinity. There can be no quality of life worth commending unless there is a reasonable standard of living to protect people from the dehumanizing ravages of deprivation, squalor, malnutrition, disease and the like. But equally – and this is what we are so slow to learn, or perhaps do not want to learn – the quality of life is a much richer concept than the standard of living. It is also much more elusive. The quality of life, because it is quality and not quantity, cannot be measured in terms of production and consumption. It has to do not with material productivity but with spiritual creativity.

It is in this all-important area that the world religions have their unique contribution to make. Whatever the differences among religions (and there are great differences) they would seem to have at least this in common, that they all stress that there is a dimension to life beyond the physical and material, and that this dimension is the pearl of great price. To lay hold on it is to enter the fullness of life; to let it slip is to be condemned to a truncated, stunted form of existence. This dimension is the holy. For some religions, the holy is concretized as a personal God. For other religions, the holy is differently understood and represented. But for all, the holy is that which has most reality and most worth.

The task common to all religions today is to commend the holy, to open to contemporary mankind this dimension which is in danger of being closed off in a world where only techniques are understood. The holy is in God, in nature, in personal relationships, in the inner depths of mystical experience. The holy is everywhere, even in our noisy and bustling cities, but we are blind to it. 'Everyday experience has within it the dimension of the holy – if we can but perceive it.'[2] The religious person sees the same world as the secular person, but he sees it differently, for he sees it in the light of the holy. This is what makes all things new, this is what confers that sense of serenity which is characteristic of the religions and likewise the sense of compassion for all beings. The vision is purified from the blinding effects of concupiscence and everywhere new potentialities are seen. The truly religious vision is never complacent, but it does have the serenity of hope, warmth, love, patience, faith in the possibility of renewal and transformation. Let me quote a Buddhist writing to express what I am trying to say: 'Here in this very chamber all the magnificent heavenly palaces and all the pure lands of all the Buddhas are manifested. This world of ours seems quite impure, replete with all kinds of woes and sorrows, wretched and full of terrors. To those, however, who have true faith, this same world appears with all the features of a pure land. . . Beings, because of their sins, cannot see the pureness of this Buddha-land of ours. Really this land of ours is ever pure. The impurities are in your own mind.'[3] As the nations today scramble and jostle for oil or metals or whatever the latest desirable commodity happens to be, do we not need the vision of planet Earth as the pure land filled with the infinite compassion of the Buddha – an Earth transformed from the one that we see through the distorting glass of greed and rivalry, but Earth as it *really* is, Earth with her potentialities fulfilled and manifesting the holiness of divine creative love?

The religions start with the disadvantage that although they have been preaching love and compassion and justice for thousands of years, it is not they that have brought about the unity (however superficial and even spurious that unity may be) of mankind but a technology which has already predisposed the contemporary mind against religion by its assumption that all problems can be solved by the magic of techniques. This is believed even about the spiritual problems of man himself. I would repeat that one cannot today be anti-technological, and would readily admit that many problems, including those that bear on man's mental and spiritual life, are to some extent at least susceptible of technical solutions, and that all the skills and objective knowledge that have accumulated need to be harnessed in such great causes as peace and justice. But the determination of goals, the decision about what is most real and most valuable, the direction of technology itself – these are not problems to be solved by techniques. The quarrel is not with technology as such, but with the mentality that it produces; though (and this is one of the frustrating ambiguities of our life today) it has to be seriously asked whether there can be large-scale technology without the pollution of the human mind by the total reliance on technique, by concupiscence, by aggression – in short, by that whole unhappy syndrome which we have already noted. We have become alert to the pollution of the environment, but a far more serious problem is the pollution of man's own mind and inner life. I believe that only religion has the spiritual dynamic needed for a radical change in human nature and human attitudes, but the nagging question remains whether we come too late. Technology and secularism are already in possession of the field, it is they that have imprinted their mark on the first phase of the emerging unitary world history, and it has become a matter of infinite difficulty to open up the dimension of the holy.

Yet one must not tamely suppose that the drift into secularism, positivism and downright materialism is irreversible. The sociologist Peter Berger agrees with the analysis given above that the rise of the modern mentality has constituted a 'profound impoverishment' of the human spirit, but he says: 'How long such a shrinkage in the scope of human experience can remain plausible is debatable.'[4] There is something like a pendulum in human history, a built-in corrective mechanism, and when men have moved too far in one direction and experience the troubles that come about through the distortion of life, then they begin to move back. Although it has happened only among a minority, the searching for a deeper spiritual life among young people in recent years is significant. It has its dangers. Perhaps most serious is the danger of superficiality and even of triviality. American students who are suddenly seized with a craze for Eastern religion are rarely prepared to wrestle with the profound and subtle ideas on which these religions are founded, and the proper study of which could occupy years of effort. Again, we are up against a characteristic of modern life which has sprung from the technological culture – namely, transience, the desire for the novel, the need to be constantly stimulated. All this militates against that very serenity which is of the essence of religion. In the extreme case, religion itself can become another sensation, along with sex, drugs and the like. *Corruptio optimi pessima*.

The danger is real, but nevertheless I believe there are grounds for real hope in the current search for religious experience. If a relation to the holy is essential to human wholeness, then people will not permit themselves to be permanently deprived of it. The quest is there, and it affords to the religions an opportunity of bringing it about that the emerging global unity will be not merely external but profoundly spiritual.

But are the religions ready to respond? When there are such great differences among them, how can they promote unity? About all that they have in common, we have seen, is a concern for the holy, and the holy itself is conceived in many different ways. The religions are today meeting and intermingling as never before. Will the result not be increased confusion?

Let me say how I see the situation. Religious truth is a dialectical matter. I use the word 'dialectical' here in a broad sense. I mean that in religion no matter what has been said, something else remains to be said; that whatever has been asserted needs to be corrected by a new assertion; that the way to truth is not through 'consensus' but through conversation and even controversy. These points seem to follow necessarily from the fact that religion is concerned with the infinite. There can be no end to the exploration of the infinite, and in that exploration one inevitably encounters paradox.

This means that one does not hold out to the modern searcher a consensus theology distilled from the living religions. The unity of the religions does not lie in any such abstraction. It is a unity that lies ahead, a unity that is coming to be as the religions encounter each other and correct each other and deepen each other. Never has the last word been said, never has any individual or group grasped in its fullness the truth of the holy. But each can help the other to notice that which has hitherto escaped notice.

I do not mean either that different religions have, as it were, different parts of the total truth. It is true that one can construct a typology of religions based on their varying insights and emphases, but it is also true that a corresponding typology can be constructed *within* each religion, for no religion is homogeneous but contains many variations. It is not that every religion has part of the truth of the holy, but that every religion has potentially the whole truth of the holy, that is to say, is moving into that truth. Religions are not static but growing. Hence in that conversation and dialogue by which they correct and enrich one another, they do so by helping one another to develop the potentialities already there, rather than through a syncretistic mingling of material.

Let me illustrate the point from Christianity. As a Christian, I believe that the truth of the holy, so far as this can be communicated to finite human minds, is adequately expressed in Jesus Christ, the incarnate Logos. But at no time has the church (and still less, individuals within the church) fully grasped this truth, or been fully grasped by it. It is a truth that is growing and deepening. One very fruitful way of learning more of that truth is the encounter with the non-Christian religions, in which the same Logos has found expression, though in a different way, perhaps even, at first sight, in a seemingly alien way. But even that which seems alien may cause me to notice in the Christian tradition elements which had hitherto been hidden but which now become clear to me as part of the growing truth. And likewise one hopes that the impact of Christianity on the non-Christian leads to a fuller understanding of that potentially whole truth which is embodied in his tradition.

Today in this large village which is planet Earth, there is a unique opportunity to bring to mankind the great resources of the religions, resources that are able to speak to every condition and type of human being. But the time is short.

13

The One and the Many: Some Implications for Religion

The distinction of the one and the many is fundamental to human experience. Both poles of this distinction seem to be equiprimordial to any intelligent awareness. 'The many' is inescapable for any experience which is spatio-temporal in its form, for the material of such an experience consists in the manifold of sensations that are spread out in space and that succeed one another in time. But to a human experience there belongs also from the beginning a unity, which allows the manifold items in it to be ordered and related among themselves, and if this did not happen, there would be no properly human experience, but only at most a chaotic flux of impressions, comparable perhaps to the flux which briefly passes through consciousness when, let us say, we are over-come by dizziness or are about to lose consciousness. At such moments, we say, the mind 'reels' and its structures seem to fall apart.

The question then might arise whether the unity of experi-ence is imposed entirely by the human mind. Is reality just that chaotic flux which we briefly glimpse in moments of dizziness and the like, and is it only our own consciousness that imposes some order upon it, giving an illusion of unity so that we can orient ourselves and survive? This might be one interpretation of Kant's epistemology, in which it is the mind which first of all imposes upon the given the forms of space and time, and then goes on to synthesize the spatio-temporal data by bringing them under the categories of understanding in the unity of apperception.

Further reflection, however, suggests that it would be impossible for the mind to impose a unity on the manifold of sensations unless the conditions for such a unity were already there in the sensations themselves. Very important, for instance, is repetition. If the flux of sensations were endlessly varied, we could never emerge from the state of dizziness nor construct any kind of unity. But in fact the same sensations keep coming back, and we are able to recognize identities. One of Kierkegaard's most obscure works was a short book called *Repetition*, and in it he drew attention to this basic factor in experience: 'When the Greeks said that all knowledge is recollection, they affirmed that all that is has been; when one says that life is a repetition, one affirms that existence which has been now becomes.'[1] It is repetition, the recurrence of what has been, that makes possible the construction of a unified experience, and this repetition lies in the given, the raw data of experience. Unity then is not a creation of the human mind, but a discovery. Still, it is a discovery which is never complete. First, the growth of common sense and then the rise and development of the sciences have more and more articulated the manifold given of experience into a whole. But every new advance has also disclosed loose ends that are unaccounted for, and if there is perception of order and unity, there seem also to be areas of randomness that resist incorporation into the unifying view.

However, the awareness of unity has come not only from the slow accumulation of knowledge and the development of the sciences. There has also been in many individuals and groups of people a mystical awareness of the underlying unity of all things. Even though particular relations were not clear, such persons have been seized of an awareness of a single Reality embracing all the manifestations of the manifold in itself and expressing itself in them. Is this to be understood as a leap ahead of the state of empirical knowledge at any given time, so as to jump across the still uncrossed territory that separates us from a vision of all things gathered up in a unity and wholeness? No, this would not be a correct way of expressing the matter. It is not just that the religious vision of unity is of a different kind from that towards which the sciences might bring us. It is rather that this vision was there at the beginning, equiprimordial as I have said with the awareness of plurality. It is not dependent upon the rise of science, but is more likely to have enabled that rise in the first place, to the extent that a prior conviction of unity was necessary to motivate the search for unifying interrelationships. It has sometimes been argued that the Judaeo-Christian belief in creation was an important factor in encouraging the rise of modern science, on the ground that this belief secularized nature and made it accessible to investigation. I have never been much impressed by this argument and regard it as, to say the least, grossly exaggerated. The influence of a doctrine of creation is to be seen more importantly in the fact that by referring all things to a single creative source, it thereby postulated from the beginning a principle of unity.

The religious vision of an all-embracing unity has found expression in various monistic philosophies. The most illustrious representative of monism in ancient Greece was Parmenides. His philosophy is rationalistic and ontological, setting little store on the deliverances of sense experience. When one chooses the rational path, then the law of self-contradiction drives inexorably toward a thoroughgoing monism. Reality is one and unchanging. That which changes is that which is not, that is to say, unreality. With the thought of Parmenides in Greece may be compared that of Sankara in India. There is one unchanging reality, Brahma. Over the face of this reality is the moving scene of *maya*, plural, differentiated, changing. But the one reality is by no means just an abstraction, for it is both real and concrete. In S. Radhakrishnan's words, 'The pure being of Brahman is not the last residue of analysis and abstraction, which is almost identical with pure nothingness, but the one Transcendent Fact within which all other facts are held. It is incomprehensible not because it is empty but because it is full.'[2] On the other side, *maya* is not just illusion. Something like a modern counterpart to these ancient monisms may be found among advocates of some forms of idealism. F. H. Bradley, for instance, believed that only the Absolute had complete reality, while all else is appearance. The very use of the term 'appearance' suggests something not quite real, though Bradley would have said about appearance what Indian philosophers have said about *maya*, namely, that it is not mere illusion. Bradley did in fact develop a difficult doctrine of degrees of reality. Reverting for a moment to ancient philosophy, we may recall something similar in the philosophy of Plotinus, which envisaged a kind of hierarchy of beings, with the One at the apex, the source and summation of reality, but with various lesser grades of reality, considered as emanations from the One.

But from the earliest times these various monistic philosophies have been opposed by others that are frankly pluralist. The opposition of monism and pluralism has in fact been 'the battle of the giants concerning Being'.[3] In ancient Greece, the priority of the multiple and the changing over the one has usually been ascribed to Heraclitus, seen as the alternative to Parmenides. Whether the two can be so simply opposed to each other is debatable. But the typical pluralist philosophy has also been empiricist, in opposition to the rationalist tendency of monism. With the rise of empiricism in modern times, pluralism has also been gaining strength. But perhaps it reached its most extreme statement in Nietzsche, who was not an empiricist, but has been seen by some as the last representative of the Western philosophical tradition. Where the monists had claimed that any contingent being is unintelligible unless we trace it back to one necessary being, Nietzsche simply accepted contingency. The world is nothing but an infinite congeries of contingent facts. They do not add up to anything or constitute any kind of unity. There is no beginning, no end, no centre, no shape or system, but just the endless proliferation of contingent occasions. This view lies at the opposite extreme from the philosophy of Parmenides, Sankara and company.

It is significant that whilst monistic philosophies tend on the whole to be religious philosophies (whether theistic, pantheistic or panentheistic), philosophies of pluralism tend to be non-religious. This is not always the case, and certainly one could not say that the religious index of a philosophy will be higher or lower, the more it tends toward monism or pluralism. For instance, William James was an enthusiastic advocate of pluralism, but he combined it with a form of theism in which he found a place for a limited God. It is true, however, that the more extreme forms of pluralism, whether based on empiricism or, as in the case of Nietzsche, on something like an existentialist basis, do tend towards an atheistic interpretation of reality. A sheer plurality of finite entities is not hospitable to God or religion.

Indeed, it can be argued that the very idea of unity is itself an important element in the concept of God. Among the many arguments that have been put forward for the existence of God at various times, one finds the so-called 'henological' argument, that is to say, the argument from the meaning (*logos*) of the one (*hen*). This argument has never had the prominence given to, let us say, the ontological or teleological arguments, but it has been recently revived and restated by Herbert Richardson.[4] Briefly, his argument is that there are three basic category systems, appropriate respectively to individuals, relations and wholes. But logic itself seeks the unity of these, the 'unity of unities', in Richardson's phrase, and this unity is what we call God.

It is interesting to note that Richardson's argument already contains something of a hint of a triune God, One in Three and Three in One. It has commonly been said by Christian theologians that whereas the existence of God can be established by philosophical reflection (natural theology), his three-in-oneness is known only through revelation. But it may be asked whether even the three-in-oneness (or, at least, the diversity in unity or possibly unity in diversity) of God is not to some extent discoverable simply through reflection on the concept of God. This explains why I have ventured to write elsewhere that 'if God had not revealed himself as triune, we would have been compelled to think of him in some such way'.[5] It also helps to explain the so-called *vestigia Trinitatis* which Christian theologians found in non-Christian religions, and which they tried to account for by ingenious if unconvincing theories of derivation. For instance, the noted

Catholic missionary, the Abbé Dubois, who lived for many years in India at the turn of the eighteenth and nineteenth centuries, was much impressed by some trinitarian aspects of Hinduism. These included the sacred syllable *aum* which, he writes, 'is composed of three letters, which in writing form only one . . . We may consider that the *a* is Brahma, the *u* Vishnu, and the *m* Siva'. Later he briefly considers the association of these three deities in the *Trimurti*, and seems to be on the verge of developing the notion of a threefold spirituality of works, faith and contemplation, such as has since been worked out in detail by Raymond Pannikar.[6] Dubois then tried to account for these relationships by a primitive revelation which had been carried through the earth by the sons of Noah in their migrations after the flood.[7] The theory seems far-fetched to us, but what is important is the recognition that the Christian doctrine of the Trinity has its reflections in non-Christian religions. This would be true not only of Hinduism, the example we have actually quoted, but of some elements in the Mahayana Buddhism. Yes, even in the Hebrew scriptures, with their almost pure monotheism, one can already see from the later Christian viewpoint the beginnings of an understanding of God as unity in diversity and diversity in unity, noticeably in such conceptions as the Word and the Spirit of the Lord and the Wisdom of God.

We come back then to the philosophical opposition between the one and the many, or between monism and pluralism, from which we set out. The notion of a triunity, or indeed of any diversity in unity and unity in diversity, overcomes the sharp opposition of monism and pluralism. Perhaps indeed it would be difficult to find anywhere a thoroughgoing monism or pluralism. For if the One is not a mere abstraction (in which case it would be hard to distinguish it from nothing) then it must contain differentiation in itself. Presumably most advocates of monism have thought of the One in this way, even if they have not explicitly said so. They have been in tacit agreement with Radhakrishnan's point, that the One is so far from being empty that it is characterized by a fullness that surpasses comprehension. At the opposite extreme, could there really be a thoroughgoing pluralism? Here even Nietzsche, who announced the death of God and denied that there is either beginning or end or middle, nonetheless taught a doctrine of eternal recurrence. Such a doctrine necessarily entails that important concept of repetition, to the fundamental importance of which I have drawn attention. Now repetition does not by itself establish an overarching unity, but it does rule out the possibility of sheer pluralism and sheer contingency. Indeed, if one were placed in such an environment, it would be impossible to say anything about it at all, for saying implies an articulation which in turn rests on repetition and identity. Thus we are bound to draw the conclusion that the extreme forms both of monism and of pluralism are untenable. The highest unity is that which already conceals within itself the richest diversity, while sheer diversity devoid of anything unifying is unthinkable. The one and the many do not stand in stark opposition to each other, for each implies the other.

In the history of religions, the same insight has usually lain not very far below the surface. Here the opposition has been between monotheism or pantheism on the one side, and polytheism with its proliferation of gods on the other. To the question, 'How many gods?' the monotheist and the pantheist have replied, 'One only.' They have maintained that the gods of polytheism are either non-existent (in the case of monotheism, with its transcendent God) or else are merely manifestations of the one immanent Being (pantheism). But these religions have to admit differentiation into their deities as soon as they reflect upon them. On the other hand, the polytheist does not worship simply a profusion of unrelated gods. These gods are in fact very closely related within a pantheon, hierarchical in its structure, so that polytheism is at least dimly aware of the unity of the divine, and in search of it.

The doctrine of the Trinity – better called the doctrine of the Triunity – and any comparable way of thinking of the divine in non-Christian religions overcomes the opposition between monotheism and polytheism and brings the notions of unity in diversity and diversity in unity in God to a new level of explicit awareness. But the history of trinitarian doctrine in the church shows how precarious is the balance that it seeks to express in its dialectic of the One in Three and Three in One. There is the constant danger of (in the terminology of the Athanasian Creed) either dividing the substance or confounding the persons, that is to say, either lapsing into tritheism or letting the distinctions be lost in a blank unity. The doctrine of the Trinity might be claimed as a theological attempt to express what philosophers have called the 'concrete universal'.

So far our discussion has been in the main theoretical, but we have to ask what all this implies for the actual life of the religions, and especially today for the ordering of relations among the great religions, as they live side by side on our small planet. I think that the practical lesson is already obvious to us, and can be drawn from the essence of religion itself in its awareness of the equiprimordiality of the one and the many and their mutual implication. In John's Gospel, Christ on the eve of his passion and death makes his great prayer for the disciples. Part of that prayer is: 'Holy Father, keep them in thy name . . . that they may be one, even as we are one' (John 17.11). Thus, the kind of unity which Christ desired for his disciples was to be like the unity between Christ himself and God the Father, the unity which later Christian theology thought out in terms of the Holy Trinity. As we have seen, this is a unity which implies diversity, so that we may neither divide the substance nor confound the differentiations within the unity.

Christ of course was thinking of his own followers, so that in the first instance his understanding of unity is applicable to the Christian church. That church through the centuries has brought forth a rich diversity of theologies, liturgies, spiritualities, life-styles, and most of these have been legitimate expressions of Christianity. They cannot be combined in some monolithic system, yet through the many variations there runs a unity which holds them together. The very extent of the variation testifies to the richness of the Christian revelation and its reception by human beings. No single variety of Christian experience expresses the full meaning of Christian faith, and even together they present only aspects, the full unification of which, so Christians believe, will come only at the end, that is to say, eschatologically. Modern ecumenists are coming more and more to recognize that the unity of the church will not be attained through a unification of structures or a series of such unifications, but that it is a much richer concept and one more difficult to define, for its model is that of the Trinity itself.

But Christ's vision for his followers may, by analogy, be extended to the whole spectrum of world religions. These religions will be living side by side on earth for the foreseeable future. They must seek to draw more closely together and demonstrate by common life and action their fundamental commitment to the One, however that One may be named in each religion. But this coming together in unity to witness to the reality of the One in face of the dissolution of society through secularism cannot be achieved either through one religion seeking to absorb another or all religions seeking to sink their differences in some colourless syncretism. It can be achieved only through a genuine unity in diversity and diversity in unity. No single faith has yet attained to understanding of the fullness of the One, even if it has the potentiality for such an understanding. Therefore each faith must be respectful towards and ready to learn from the spiritual insights of others. Even so the One and the many as a principle of ontology can be reflected in the actual life of the communities of faith.

14

Commitment and Openness: The Christian and Other Faiths

The subject of the relation of Christianity to other faiths is one that arouses much interest at the present time. There are many reasons for this. Some people in Western countries, disillusioned with much in their own culture, have been discovering or rediscovering the depth and wisdom of Eastern religions. The vastly increased opportunities for travel and even for migration are bringing people of different backgrounds into touch with one another as never before. The scriptures of the great world religions have become easily accessible in paperback translations. Departments of religious studies in modern universities have been very popular, and seem to offer a breadth of interest surpassing the narrower fields of study in the older faculties of Christian theology. All this new interest in the spectrum of the world's religions is to be welcomed. Yet the very fascination of the subject must not blind us to the difficulties that lie in the way of working out a satisfactory relationship among the religions. So I shall begin with a few cautionary points, in which I draw attention to some of the pitfalls that lie in the way of those who wish to take up this question.

First of all, we have to be aware of the complexity and sophistication that characterize the great religions: Buddhism, Islam and the others. Too many people in the West, including Christian theologians, have ventured to talk about them and even to write about them without doing all the necessary homework. Just as a full acquaintance with Christianity, its history, scriptures, theology, worship and so on, needs years of study, so does a full acquaintance with any of the other great religions of the world. Perhaps a single scholar can become really proficient in only one religion other than his own – one thinks for instance of Kenneth Cragg who has spent years in deepening his knowledge of Islam and in establishing links between Islam and Christianity. By contrast, there is something like a lack of respect for the non-Christian religions in those writers who skip rapidly from Christianity to Islam to Hinduism to Shintoism and back again in an exercise which is often far too superficial and not really helpful in promoting better relations among the religions.

Second, I think we have to guard against the danger of acquiring too academic an understanding of non-Christian religions. Western scholars tend, for instance, to study the classical texts of Hinduism and to engage in discussion with professors in Hindu universities. But this procedure might be as misleading as forming an opinion of Christianity based on the utterances of the Oxford theology faculty. Not enough attention is paid to the many levels of religion, and especially popular religion, both Christian and non-Christian. Spiritual insights are often gained first of all on the level of myth and cult, and are only later refined in the concepts of theology and philosophy, and even so, something of the substance may be lost in the process.

Third, it is important that we in the West get away from the idea that we are doing something new when we engage in dialogue with Buddhism, Hinduism and the rest. We could of course, remind ourselves that as early as the second century Justin the Martyr wrote a *Dialogue with Trypho, a Jew*, but since we are thinking chiefly of the Eastern religions, what I have in mind is the fact that in many Asian countries Christians and non-Christians have now been living side by side for centuries, they have been in relation and dialogue, and in most cases they have worked out some *modus vivendi*. In this connection, the Japanese Christian scholar, Yasuo Furuya, has recently written: 'When you Western Christians become fascinated with Eastern religions, I wish you would show at least a matching interest in Asian Christianity and

Asian Christians. For we have been living with Eastern religions for centuries, not merely on a theoretical but on a daily practical level. Accordingly, while you are excited about dialogue with other religions, I wish you would have dialogue with your fellow Christians.'[1] Dr Furuya goes on to reinforce a point which I made earlier, namely, the superficiality that often attends Western Christian statements about Eastern religions. He writes: 'Buddhism is as vast and complicated a subject to study as Christianity, if not more so. We oriental Christians are surrounded by many Buddhist scholars and specialists who point out the ignorance, misunderstanding, generalization and oversimplification often made by Western theologians. By contrast, Asian Christian theologians know what the real issues are, especially the vulnerable points on each side.'[2] We would do well then to pay more attention than we usually do to voices from Asian Christianity before plunging into direct dialogue with the ancient Asian religions.

If we pay attention to these warning signs that I have set up, I think we may now go on to reject two very one-sided views of the relation of Christianity to other faiths. These two views have each had distinguished advocates, but I do not think that either of them stands up to serious criticism.

The first of these one-sided conceptions of Christianity's relation to other religions is what may be called the 'exclusivist' view. According to this view, there is no truth, no genuine relation to God, to be found outside of the Christian faith. This view has always had its representatives, and the most famous in recent times was Karl Barth. He based his case chiefly on a distinction between religion and revelation. 'In religion,' he claimed, 'man ventures to grasp at God.'[3] It is seen by Barth as a purely human attempt to reach to an understanding of God, and he believes that it can lead only into error. It is the opposite of revelation, in which God reaches out to man and makes himself known. This outreach of God, the true revelation, has occurred, so Barth believed, only in the biblical and Christian tradition. But I do not believe myself that Barth's distinction between religion and revelation is a valid one. The non-Christian religions too testify that what they claim to know of God has come to them from God's self-communication, and is not just human projection or human speculation. If one were to contest this claim, there would be needed first of all an exhaustive knowledge of all the great religious traditions of the world, something which Barth certainly did not have. Something even more than that would be needed – an Olympian standpoint outside history from which an absolute judgment upon the several traditions could be delivered, and no human being is or could be in a position to make such an absolute judgment.

Few modern theologians have gone quite so far as Barth in their dismissal of the non-Christian religions. But we have to note that even some of those who at first sight may seem more liberal may have prejudged important issues, so that they have not in fact moved very far from the exclusivist position. Paul Tillich, for instance, was ready to acknowledge that all religions, Christian and non-Christian alike, are the recipients of revelation. But this apparent generosity was undercut by the distinction that he made between preparatory revelation and final revelation. He tells us that 'all religions and cultures outside the Church are still in the period of preparation'.[4] Christianity alone has received the final revelation. Thus while Tillich has departed from the cruder forms of exclusivism, he still makes a very sharp judgment on the difference of quality between the Christian revelation and all other alleged revelations, and this judgment seems to be quite as arbitrary as Barth's. At the end of his life, however, Tillich adopted a more generous stance. The Roman Catholic theologian Karl Rahner also appears to show generosity through his willingness to bestow the title of 'anonymous Christian'[5] upon serious-minded adherents of other faiths or even of secular ideologies. But there is a kind of Christian imperialism concealed in this attempt to assimilate Buddhist or Muslim or Marxist virtue under the Christian umbrella. In fact, all of these represent distinctive ideals of humanity. As another Roman Catholic theologian, Hans Küng, has remarked in opposition to Rahner, 'only a naive ignorance of the facts makes it possible to overlook or assimilate the distinctive qualities of each one'.[6] So we have to be on our guard against exclusivism not only in its forth-right expression but also in a variety of veiled forms.

At the opposite extreme from exclusivism there is an equally unsatisfactory position. This is the position of a thoroughgoing relativism. On this view, all the great religions are held to be equally valid. Each expresses the religiosity of a particular culture, and is the appropriate expression of religion for those who happen to be at home in that culture. John Hick seems to come pretty close to such a view when he declares that 'it is not appropriate to speak of a religion being true or false, any more than it is to speak of a civilization as being true or false . . . the same differences between the eastern and western minds, expressed in different conceptual and linguistic, social, political and artistic forms, presumably underlie the contrasts between eastern and western forms of religion'.[7]

In fairness to Hick, it ought to be said that this denial of truth and falsity in religion seems to be modified elsewhere in his writings, where he distinguishes between 'two aspects of a religion . . . its central affirmations concerning the nature of reality, and the mythology with its often poetic elaborations and its concrete cultic expressions'.[8] He acknowledges that the former are ultimately true or false, but sees the latter as cultural products. This looks very much like an example of the tendency to despise popular religion and to undervalue the importance of myth as a possible way of expressing truth. When, for instance, one compares the biblical myth of creation with, let us say, one of the Gnostic myths on the same theme, this is not just a case of setting side by side two stories from different cultural backgrounds. The two myths teach contradictory doctrines about the material world. The biblical story teaches that the material world is good and promotes an affirmative attitude towards it, the Gnostic myth teaches that it is evil and that therefore salvation consists in escaping from the entanglements of matter. It is possible, of course, that both teachings might be false, but what is logically impossible is that they are both true. A question of truth and falsity does arise in religion, even at the level of myth and cult, and to opt for one alternative or the other is to make a judgment about what is true, not just to express a cultural preference.

It is of course true that there are profound affinities among the great religions of the world, and that these affinities may at first be obscured by the cultural forms in which they are expressed. But there are also – as we noted already in criticizing Rahner's idea of the anonymous Christian – profound differences, which amount in some cases to contradictions. The religions cannot be merged together in some syncretistic cosmic faith. That would do scant justice to the distinctive contributions which each brings. The easy-going tolerance which hails the religions as all equally true, or even denies that the question of truth arises, is far too simplistic. What is needed is a patient uncovering of the points of agreement and conflict. Sometimes it may be possible to resolve the conflicts in a more comprehensive truth, but sometimes also it will be necessary to come down on one side or the other. This is the long and sometimes painful process of dialogue among the religions, and we shall say more about it later. But for the present, I think it has become clear to us that in the question of Christianity's relation to other faiths, the position of extreme relativism has to be rejected just as firmly as the exclusivist position.

What then is the position which I would commend? I shall describe it by the compound expression, 'openness and commitment'. Assuredly, this is much more difficult than the two rather simplistic positions which I have criticized. The demand for openness follows from our rejection of the exclusivist point of view. The demand for commitment follows similarly from our dissatisfaction with a thorough-going relativism. But is not the combination of openness and commitment a contradiction? I do not think so, though its working out in detail is far from easy. To begin with, I think we may say that both commitment and openness are demanded of us by the limitations of the human condition itself, and to some extent we have already taken note of this in the earlier part of the chapter. If no one can ever attain a really deep and intimate knowledge of more than one or two of the great religious traditions, then he must always be

open to the possibility of learning new religious truths that
have not thitherto come to his notice. Certainly he cannot
pronounce negative judgments on religious systems about
which he knows very little. Yet I do not want to suggest that
it is merely a matter of refraining from negative judgments,
for I think that the limited amount that each of us may know
about other religions encourages us to believe that there is
much more of value waiting to be discovered. On the other
hand, the same limitations drive us to a specific commitment.
As finite beings, we are limited in our knowledge, limited
in our time and energy, limited by our culture and historical
situation which make it inevitable that we see things from
one perspective rather than another. We cannot follow all
the paths at once, otherwise we become mere dilettantes and
dabblers. In religion, syncretism has usually led to superficiality and sentimentalism. Whereas John Hick has
commended what he calls a 'global theology', drawing on
all the religious traditions,[9] I have myself written of 'the
impossible ideal of a universal philosophical theology, that
is to say, one that would look along all perspectives and
would gather up all revelation, all experiences and all
symbols of the holy. This is an impossible ideal for man as
a being who is "there", at a particular time and place in
history. If the ideal is possible for anyone, it could only be
for a god or maybe an angel.'[10] It is therefore necessary for
those who disclaim to being either gods or angels to commit
themselves to a particular tradition and to enter into it in
depth. The result of this will not be the kind of fanaticism
or exclusivism that I have already condemned. To take a
tradition as definitive is not to absolutize it in an illegitimate
way. On the contrary, by entering in depth into one
tradition, one may well be for the first time convinced of the
depth that lies in all the great religious traditions.

Some such position as the one that I have described by
the expression 'commitment and openness' is the only one
that makes a genuine dialogue among the religions possible.
The precondition of any dialogue is that those who engage
in it have some common ground that makes communication
possible, but also that they have some differences that make

their dialogue worthwhile. If one went along with the exclusivist view, dialogue would be impossible, while on the basis
of a thoroughgoing relativism, dialogue would be otiose.

It is, I think, in enabling dialogue that the position of
openness and commitment is put to the practical test. The
underlying assumption brought to the dialogue is, I think,
not so much that each religious tradition is a broken light, a
fragment of some great whole that can be pieced together
with the other fragments into a whole, as rather that each
tradition is a kind of organism that already has the possibility
of growing into the whole, sometimes by developing, sometimes by discarding, its existing features. Along with that
goes the acknowledgment that never at any moment in
history has one's tradition attained its potential wholeness.

To put this in Christian terms, a Christian committed to
his faith may take that faith as definitive and believe that in
Christ there is the fullness of truth. But he would have to
say that neither he as an individual nor the Christian church
in its corporate life has ever fully comprehended this truth.
He would therefore be open to learn more of the truth of
Christ, even to deepen his Christian commitment, through
his contacts with non-Christian religions, or even secular
ideologies. This is what the Roman Catholic theologian of
religions, H. R. Schlette, had in mind when he wrote: 'The
non-Christian religion brings its contribution not as something extraneous but as an extension and enrichment of
catholicity itself, which is never absolute or perfect.'[11] Thus,
to give examples, it may be from Islam that the Christian
learns the importance of racial solidarity, or it may be from
Hinduism that he learns the virtue of non-violence. Yet in
both cases he is not learning something foreign to his own
tradition, but rather is being awakened to elements in that
tradition which he had hitherto neglected. This may happen
in the other direction, when the Christian brings to
consciousness in the non-Christian religion something that
is not foreign but the awakening of a potentiality in the
tradition itself. An example of this would be the rise of
nineteenth-century reforming movements in Hinduism,
which were evoked by the Christian presence in India but

found an adequate ground for development within Hinduism. The process I have described is similar to what the American philosopher Ernest Hocking called 'reconception'. 'One's conceptions,' he wrote, 'have been inadequate; they have not anticipated new vistas and motives: we require to understand our own religion better – we must *reconceive* it – then we shall see how the new perspectives belong quite naturally to what has always been present in its nature, unnoticed or unappreciated by us.'[12] He goes on to claim that through this process there will come about a growing resemblance among the religions, yet, 'the process does tend to a decision, not through a conflict of faiths or a campaign for world dominance, but through the unforced persuasiveness of relative success in this effort to become a better vehicle of truth'.[13]

It might seem that there are two items in the Christian tradition that stand in the way of the dialogue, development and even reconception of which I have been speaking. I mean the doctrine of incarnation and the command to mission. Do these not constitute an insuperable barrier in the way of developing better relations between Christianity and other faiths?

Let me begin by saying something about incarnation. That God was in Christ, that he has sent forth his Son, that the Word has been made flesh, are central affirmations of the New Testament and of the Christian faith. The ideas lying behind such language are, of course, highly complex, and even down to our own day theologians have occupied themselves finding new and more illuminating ways of interpreting the mystery of God in Christ. No doubt there are some ways of interpreting the belief in incarnation which do destroy the possibility of dialogue with other faiths. If the claim is made that in Jesus Christ and in him alone there is any genuine knowledge of God, then all other religions are implicitly dismissed as fabrications. This, as we have seen, was the view of Karl Barth, but I have tried to show that it is not one that is securely founded and that it ought to be rejected. But if the Christian is saying that in Jesus Christ he finds the definitive focus of God's acting and presence in the world – an acting and presence which are also universal – then there is much less of a barrier.

Indeed, there is no barrier at all, but rather another powerful incentive to dialogue. For the idea of incarnation is not peculiar to Christianity. Parallels to a doctrine of incarnation are found in other faiths. The doctrine of incarnation is so far from being one that Christians ought to abandon in order to cultivate relations with other faiths that it can rather provide material for mutual exploration at the deepest level, for incarnation is one of the most profound ideas that have ever arisen in the history of religion. It speaks of a God who is not just creator, ruler, lawgiver, judge, but of a God who cares and who, in his intimate concern for his creatures, has gone to the length of identifying with them. And this is not just a general truth, as some Hegelian philosophers were willing to say, but one that fulfils itself in the concreteness of history. The idea of a descent or *avatar* of the gods is familiar in Hindu thought. Vishnu had ten such incarnations, Siva no less than twenty-eight! The most beloved figure in the popular religion of India, as distinct from the philosophical religion of the learned, is Krishna, an incarnation of Vishnu. In the famous lines of the *Bhagavadgita*, the motive for incarnation is expressed:

'Whensoever the law fails and lawlessness arises,
I bring myself to embodied birth. To guard the righteous,
I come to birth age after age.'[14]

One might also mention the Buddhist belief in *bodhisattvas* who give up their own salvation to return again and again to earth to labour for the salvation of mankind. One such popular figure is represented in Japanese religious art as the Buddha of the thousand arms – he needs all these arms for his saving work. Of course, these Hindu and Buddhist examples are not identical with the Christian doctrine of incarnation, but they do provide common ground rather than a barrier, and they all enrich the understanding of deity by their stress on the love of God and even his sufferings with his creatures. When I was giving a seminar in India some years ago on christology, a member of the group said one day: 'In India, christology is possible only as Krish-nology.' I am still trying to work out the implications of this remark, but I think it does open up a vast area of dialogue which can be helpful to Christians and non-Christians alike.

What about mission? Is that not a stumbling block on the Christian side to any genuine dialogue? Certainly one would have to agree that mission belongs to the essence of Christianity. One can no more excise from Christianity its missionary vocation than one can excise the doctrine of incarnation – in either case, the result would be a mutilation that would probably prove to be mortal. Let us remember too that other religions besides Christianity are missionary. No doubt it is only natural that if people believe that they are attaining salvation or enlightenment through a religious faith, they will desire to communicate this faith to others and share its advantages. But to speak in this way is to suggest that the motive for mission is altruistic, whereas it has in fact often been the expansionist drive of a community or institution. Still, the abuse of mission does not invalidate the possibility of a right use. There is at present much rethinking on the subject of Christian mission. If it is seen in terms of converting people of other faiths to the Christian religion, then undoubtedly it stands as a barrier to any dialogue or to any relations of friendship and co-operation. But it can be argued that the deepest motive for mission – and this would be true not only of the Christian mission but of the missions of other religions – is the enhancement of human life. This is more fundamental than any institutional expansion. Some words that John's Gospel attributes to Jesus are significant: 'I came that they may have life and have it abundantly' (John 10.10). This is how his own mission or sending into the world was understood.

If we bear in mind this fundamental understanding of mission, then we see that mission can take various forms. These may be different at different times in history and in different circumstances. I think the Christian mission today can be understood in ways which do not constitute a barrier in the *rapprochement* with other faiths. There are at least three possibilities. In many cases, the traditional method of proclamation aimed at eliciting a Christian commitment is still appropriate. Although we have been thinking in this chapter about the higher ethical religions, there has been much bad religion in the world that distorts human life. There are also today inhuman ideologies and a great deal of irresponsible self-indulgence. No apology is necessary if the Christian mission seeks to bring such people to an acceptance of Christian faith. On the other hand, in the case of those who adhere to one of the other great world religions, then I would think that mission should take the form of dialogue as I have described it earlier in this chapter – a conversation in which each speaks and each listens, each gives and each learns, each is prepared to reconceive his beliefs and practices in the light of the other, but without abandoning his own tradition. There is still a third form of mission, where neither proclamation nor dialogue is appropriate. By this third form, I mean simply silent presence and service among those who need it. Probably the greatest Christian missionary in the world today is Mother Teresa. As far as I am aware, she does not proclaim the gospel to crowds packed into a sports stadium; she does not engage in academic dialogue with Buddhist or Hindu professors; but she does befriend the dying and the outcasts of Calcutta, and if mission means helping to enhance life, then that is as assuredly mission as any of the other forms.

The new relationship between Christianity and other faiths is only at a beginning, after centuries in which there has been little communication other than polemic. But already there are many promising features in the relationship, and the whole picture may be very much transformed in the coming decades.

15

The Church and the Ministry

(i) Ministerial functions

We often hear it said that the Christian minister today is in search of an image. For many centuries, he had a unique and honoured place in society, but even in the last generation there has been a rapid erosion of his position, though the conditions for this critical deterioration had been building up for a long time. With the secularization of society, many of the functions once performed by Christian priests or ministers have been taken over by others – educationists, social workers, psychoanalysts, counsellors of various sorts. Even within the church, the new stress on the responsibility of the laity has led some to question whether a full-time ministry or even an ordained ministry of any kind is necessary.

This radical questioning may, however, lead to good results if it forces us to look beyond the sociological accidents of ministry to its theological essence. At any given time, the form of Christian ministry is determined partly by the cultural factors operating in the society into which it happens to be inserted, partly by the theological givens that lie at the root of the ministry. How many different kinds of bishop, for instance, there have been from the days of the pagan Roman Empire down to twentieth-century America! We may believe that through the many changes the apostolic commission has continued, but often enough the theological meaning of ministry has been obscured or even come near to disappearing under the cultural trappings. The eighteenth-century English bishop who stayed in London for nine months of the year so that he might fulfil his duties in the House of Lords, chiefly by supporting the party that had appointed him to his see, is not easily recognizable as a successor of the apostles. So it is no bad thing when the Christian minister is, from time to time, compelled to reconsider his fundamental *raison d'être*.

This means that we have to consider ministry in relation to the church, bearing in mind that the church, though it is a human institution and therefore susceptible to sociological analysis, is more than a *merely* human institution. It has originated in the calling of God, it is a sign in the midst of the world pointing forward to the Kingdom of God and is therefore in its deepest significance a mystery demanding a theological rather than a sociological approach.

It is in the context of this theological entity, the church, that we must seek to understand the Christian ministry. As Hans Küng has remarked, it is possible to 'discern both constants and variables in the ministry'.[1] For the most part, the constants are theological, though of course even in the theology of ministry a development of understanding can take place. The variables belong mainly to the changing cultural settings. These variables are highly important if the ministry is to be effective, but they are so diverse even in the many environments within a single great metropolis that the question of effectively inserting Christian ministry into any given situation is a highly particular and individualized one. I shall be concerned mainly with the constants, recognizing that they will appear differently and be differently weighted in different situations.

But there is another reason for concentrating on these constants. As the position of the ministry in society at large has been increasingly threatened, there has been an attempt, understandable enough, to make it look as much as possible like some of the secular professions that seem to be competing with it. Christian ministers today are tempted to imitate the roles of more prestigious members of society, to become like social workers or clinical psychologists or even business executives. It is right certainly that in the modern exercise of ministry, those engaged in it should learn as much as they can from experts in many fields and should work with them in matters of common concern. But no satisfying image of the ministry will be reached by merely imitating, often in an amateurish way, the psychologist or whoever it may be. The Christian minister has his own distinctive functions and these must finally be determinative. These distinctive functions have a theological basis, they assume that there is a reality we call God, that the church has a dimension of being that goes beyond the human, that in Jesus Christ there is a salvation and wholeness that no merely secular agency can provide. Daniel Day Williams once wrote: 'To bring salvation to the human spirit is the goal of all Christian ministry.'[2] This puts in a sentence the distinctive work of Christian ministry, the fundamental constant which remains through all the variables. But if the basic theological assumptions of ministry, the beliefs which motivate it, have become eroded, then there is no future for Christian ministry. Better training, more up-to-date methods, knowledge of psychology or sociology, more efficient organization – all these will accomplish nothing of importance if we have lost confidence in the thing itself, the fundamental task of bringing to human beings the proffered salvation of God.

We come back, then, to ministry in the church, which is indeed a people, a community of human beings, but a people of God, a community having a depth and significance which must be traced beyond the human to God himself. The whole church, as the people of God, has a ministry and priesthood. 'You are a chosen race, a royal priesthood, a holy nation, God's own people' (1 Peter 2.9). We should notice that this ministry and priesthood belong to the people as a whole. It is understood collectively. It is a mistaken individualism and egalitarianism that talks about the 'priesthood of all believers', as if this priesthood of the people could be divided up into equal shares among all the members of the people. All do share in it, but they do so in different ways. We must never separate ministry and church, for the ministry is to be understood in the context of the church. But likewise we must not simply absorb the distinctive ordained ministry into the general ministry of the whole church. The very idea of the church as the people of God or the body of Christ implies that from the beginning the church had a differentiated organic structure or order, for a people is not a collection of individuals all alike nor is a body an assemblage of identical organs. Both ideas imply differentiation within the over-arching unity.

The *Report on Doctrine in the Church of England (1938)*, which still gets cited in official ecumenical documents and which seems therefore to be acquiring the reputation of offering something like a classic statement, puts the matter thus: 'There was not first an apostolate which gathered a body of believers about itself; nor was there a completely structureless body of believers which gave authority to the apostles to speak and act on its behalf. To suppose that the organization of the Church must have begun in one or other of these ways is to misconceive the situation. From the first, there was the fellowship of believers finding its unity in the Twelve. Thus the New Testament bears witness to the principle of a distinctive ministry, as an original element, but not the sole constitutive element in the life of the church.'[3] This finds an echo in the Anglican-Roman Catholic agreed statement on ministry, where we read that the ordained ministry 'is not an extension of the common Christian priesthood but belongs to another realm of the gifts of the Spirit'.[4] Similarly the dogmatic constitution on the church (*Lumen Gentium*) of Vatican II declares that while the common priesthood of the faithful and ministerial priesthood are interrelated, 'they differ from one another in essence and not only in degree'.[5] Admittedly there are some obscurities in these statements, and we shall have to examine more closely the question of how the ordained ministry differs from the general ministry. But the fact that there is a difference has been clearly recognized from the time of the Gospels, in which the Twelve receive their ministry directly from Christ and not from the church at large, right down to the modern documents just quoted.

It is a case, however, of making a distinction without making a division. Though the ordained ministry is distinctive, it is exercised in the context of the church and cannot, so to speak, go it alone. This has been clearly recognized in recent years by the stress laid on collegiality – of the Pope with the bishops, of the bishops with the clergy, and of the ordained with the whole company of the faithful. Christian ministry cannot be exercised outside of this collegial context. On the other hand, as ecumenical considerations have shown, it must be admitted that on particular occasions it may not be clear just how far the context extends. It may sometimes happen that what appears to be an isolated act of ministry apart from the context of the church as understood in a legal or institutional way could claim to be within the ecclesial context if understood in a broader sacramental sense. Any such claims would have to be judged on the peculiar circumstances of each case.

But now let me set out, in fairly broad strokes, what may be called in Küng's useful terminology the 'constants' of the ministry, those basic functions which the ordained have performed from the beginning through all the changes that the centuries have brought. Since all ministry is the gift of Christ to his church and a participation in his own ministry, we can see the basic functions of Christian ministry most clearly by looking first at Christ's own ministry as portrayed in the New Testament. I think we can group the functions of that ministry under three main headings.

The first is the serving function. To say this might seem at first glance a mere tautology, for is not all ministry service and is not that simply what the word 'ministry' means? The Greek word used for 'ministry' in the New Testament is *diakonia*, 'service'. But the tautology has to be uttered, because one of the most unfortunate effects of the dominance of sociological over theological factors in Christian ministry has been the obscuring of the servant function, especially in ages of clericalism. To be sure, one could never get away from the linguistic fact that ministry means service, and the Pope has for long had as one of his titles 'Servant of the servants of God'. But there have been many times in history when the application of this title must have seemed ironical in the extreme.

Certainly the ministry of Jesus was one of service and this is what he demanded of his disciples also. He said: 'You know that those who are supposed to rule over the Gentiles lord it over them, and their great men exercise authority over them. But it shall not be so among you; but whoever would be great among you must be your servant, and whoever would be first among you must be slave of all. For the Son of man also came not to be served but to serve, and to give his life as a ransom for many' (Mark. 10.42–45). In John's Gospel we read: 'You call me teacher and Lord; and you are right, for so I am. If I then your Lord and teacher have washed your feet, you also ought to wash one another's feet. For I have given you an example, that you also should do as I have done to you' (John 13.13–15). It was natural that in the first christological thinking of the early church, the image of the suffering servant from Isaiah came to be applied to Jesus Christ. In the great christological passage of Paul's letter to the Philippians, it is said that Christ emptied himself, 'taking the form of a servant' (Phil. 2.7), and the word here translated 'servant' is *doulos*, a word signifying the abasement of a very slave.

It is right that one of the ancient orders of ministry in the Christian church should bear the name 'diaconate', for it focusses and symbolizes for us the obscure unspectacular service that is very much at the heart of Christian ministry. The deacon gets no publicity and has no prestige; he is simply an attendant belonging to what is often considered an inferior order of ministry. Perhaps it is our unwillingness to be merely obscure servants that has led to the decline of the diaconate and its reduction to a temporary stage in ministry, and perhaps there can be no healthy Christian ministry until the diaconate has been restored and its true serving functions rediscovered.

But can we spell out in more detail the kind of service demanded of Christian ministry? Again, we look to Jesus Christ, and we find that his service was above all directed to the sick, the handicapped, the outcasts and rejects of society. His was a ministry of healing in the broadest sense, of bringing wholeness, that is to say, salvation, to those whose lives had been blighted for whatever reason. It is the same service to human need that remains basic to ministry today. Paul broadened the idea of a ministry of healing to the more general idea of a ministry of reconciliation (II Cor. 5.19). Jesus had himself set the precedent by combining acts of healing with declarations of forgiveness. It is reconciliation that is distinctive of Christian ministry – reconciliation of those who are estranged from each other, reconciliation of those who are split within themselves, reconciliation of all to God. To be sure, there can be no superficial reconciliation that does not go to the roots of what has divided and deal with that, in a drastic way if necessary. But even through struggle the Christian always looks to final reconciliation, and this is what differentiates his approach from that of others, such as Marxists, who also profess a concern for the victims of society.

Another note in the serving ministry of Christ is his suffering – he is the suffering servant. Suffering is inseparable from ministry. Sometimes, indeed, all that the Christian minister can do is stand with the other, sharing his suffering and absorbing something of it. It will not be forgotten that the words of Christ, quoted above, about coming not to be served but to serve, ended with the saying that he would give his life as a ransom for many. These words give us a glimpse of the depth of commitment demanded in ministerial service, and though there are relatively few who make that response in its full depth by literally giving their lives in martyrdom, I think we have all known some saintly ministers who have truly spent themselves in service.

We often hear nowadays the expression 'enabling ministry', and this describes very well the kind of service we have been trying to envisage. The enabler does not impose solutions nor does he obtrude his own agency. Rather, he helps people and groups of people to come to themselves and to find reconciliation before God, just as in the Gospels we see Jesus bringing out the best possibilities in those whom he meets. This is by no means a passive ministry; it is an active and costly one, but it is a self-effacing one. It is a ministry of what I call 'letting-be' in the strong sense of that expression – for what more can be done for anyone than simply to let that person *be* in all the fullness of being?

But now we turn to a different group of ministerial functions, and at first sight they may seem to contradict what has just been said about service. In the Gospels, Jesus appears as the suffering servant, but equally he appears as the authoritative teacher. 'They were astonished at his teaching, for he taught them as one who had authority, and not as the scribes' (Mark 1.22). In the Sermon on the Mount, he fearlessly revises the law of Moses: 'You have heard that it was said to the men of old . . . but I say to you . . . (Matt. 5.21–22). In some of his parables and sayings he suggests that men's eternal destiny will be determined by their response to himself. He speaks out against the religious establishment of his day, he overthrows the tables of the money changers and cleanses the Temple of those who had commercialized it. All this too is ministry, but it shows new aspects of ministry, different from those which we considered under the heading of service. This second major aspect of ministry, with its inevitable accompaniment of authority, may be designated in a general way as proclamation.

Jesus himself came into Galilee, 'preaching the gospel of God' (Mark 1.14). At the end of his career, the disciples continued this ministry of proclamation, for 'they went forth and preached everywhere' (Mark 16.20). The proclamation has authority not because of those who proclaim it but because, as they believe, it is a message from God which they are commissioned to preach to human beings everywhere.

Proclamation is by no means opposed to service within the total context of ministry. Indeed, each needs the other. There are times when the silent witness of service is the best way of commending the gospel and communicating the message of salvation, but a time must come when it is necessary to articulate that gospel in words. On the other hand, a mere proclamation that was unaccompanied by service would verge on hypocrisy.

Proclamation itself is of several kinds. It may be directed to those outside the church and take the form of evangelism

– and such was the nature of the first preaching. Or it may be directed to those within the church for their upbuilding and instruction in the faith, and then it becomes part of the church's teaching office or *magisterium*. Or again, there is prophetic preaching, which may be directed either to the church or to society at large, and which subjects both church and society to the critique of God's word.

When we discussed service earlier on, it would perhaps have been difficult to say how the service of the ordained in the cause of reconciliation differs from the service of all who belong to the people of God. But the ministry of proclamation is more distinctively a part of ordained ministry or at least of a form of ministry that requires training and commissioning. In fact, among the Lutherans, proclamation or preaching is the great work of ministry and the right to preach is very carefully safeguarded. However, it would be wrong to make preaching exclusively the prerogative of the ordained, as if one could neatly divide Christians into an *ecclesia docens* and an *ecclesia discens*. We are all, in a sense, teachers and all, in a sense, learners, inasmuch as we can all help each other to deeper faith and understanding. To think out the meaning of the Christian message for today and then to proclaim it is a task that demands the co-operation and shared insights of bishops, parish clergy, theologians and lay people in the work that I have elsewhere called 'co-theologizing' and which I regard as equally important alongside the related ideas of collegiality and concelebration. All of these demonstrate in actual practice the interrelatedness of all ministry within the church, though they should not blur proper distinctions. Again, we must remember that while bishops and other ordained ministers must be willing to hear and learn from their lay brothers and sisters, they have a special responsibility of leadership in maintaining the purity of the church's proclamation and witness. Sometimes in the prevailing egalitarian atmosphere one fears that those who ought to be leading the church are running away from the ministry of proclamation and teaching with all its weight of responsibility, and by so doing are creating bewilderment among many lay people. If the word 'deacon' stresses service in the ministry, the words 'bishop' and 'presbyter', that is to say, 'overseer' and 'elder', summon the ministry to the acceptance of a leadership role, necessary in any community.

I come finally to a third group of ministerial functions, and these are the priestly functions. In some ways, these priestly functions sum up in themselves and unite the two aspects of service and proclamation already considered. For the priest is essentially a mediator, a representative who can face both ways and relate two parties. The priest represents the church in humility before God and represents also God's word to his church.

We have taken note that there is a priesthood that belongs to the whole church. But within the church there is a special exercise of priesthood belonging to bishops and presbyters. This again is a sharing in the priestly ministry of Christ, and we must go back to that for an understanding.

There are several passages in the New Testament where Christ is represented as a priest, either explicitly or implicitly. At the beginning of the Revelation of St John the Divine, the risen Christ dramatically appears to the author, clad in shining priestly garments, with a message for the church, for which he has died and for which he remains infinitely concerned. The Epistle to the Hebrews makes much more extended use of the idea of the priesthood of Christ. This priesthood is explicitly contrasted with the priesthood of the Old Testament. The sacrifices of animals could never take away sin, but Christ, our High Priest, has offered the sacrifice of himself. He is both priest and victim, the true mediator who has rent the veil of the Temple and opened a way into the presence of God. This new transcendent priesthood of Christ is compared by the writer to the eternal priesthood of Melchizedek. Then there is the great high-priestly prayer in John's Gospel. Here Christ intercedes for his own as he approaches the time of death and sacrifice. And with this may be compared the similar image in the same gospel of Christ as the good shepherd who gives his life for the sheep, the chief pastor of the flock for which he sheds his blood.

It is sometimes said that in these New Testament passages the name of priest is reserved to Christ alone, and that it was an illegitimate extension of this usage when the terms came to be applied to Christian ministry in the church. The church as a whole, of course, is called a 'royal priesthood', so that some participation in Christ's priesthood is possible for all his followers. Also, while the Epistle to the Hebrews applies the word 'priest' only to Christ, A. H. Baverstock makes the point that the very title of High Priest implies that others are associated with him in his priesthood.[6] A somewhat clearer picture emerges in John's Gospel, in the high-priestly prayer. That prayer falls into three parts. First, Jesus prays for himself, as the climax of his ministry approaches. Then he prays for the Twelve whom the Father has given him out of the world, and his prayer is: 'Sanctify them in the truth . . . for their sake I consecrate myself, that they may also be consecrated in truth' (John 17;17–19). The verb here translated 'sanctify' or 'consecrate' is in Greek *hagiazo*, and this same verb has been used in an earlier chapter of the Gospel which speaks of Christ as him 'whom the Father consecrated and sent into the world' (John 10.36). There seems here to be a parallel between the consecration and sending of Christ and the consecration and sending of the Twelve. And since the third part of the great prayer intercedes for the church as a whole, for those who would believe through the word of the Twelve, it seems clear that we have to do with a special priestly participation granted to the apostles as distinct from the participation belonging to the whole body of the faithful. Finally,if one adds at this point also the good shepherd image, there is no question but that Peter and his colleagues were also shepherds, and indeed the word 'pastor' has become one of the commonest designations of an ordained minister.

Thus, in a special way, bishops and presbyters share a priesthood derived from Christ. In the words of the agreed Anglican-Roman Catholic statement on ministry, 'despite the fact that in the New Testament ministers are never called priests (*hiereis*), Christians came to see the priestly role of Christ reflected in these ministers and used priestly terms in describing them. . . . So our two traditions commonly use priestly terms in speaking about the ordained ministry.'[7]

But what specifically are these priestly functions of the ministry? They are associated above all with the Christian sacraments in which the Christian priest represents Christ to the people and acts in his name. In baptism and confirmation, the bishop or presbyter acts to incorporate a member into Christ's body and to commission that person to a participation in the mission and ministry of the whole church. In the sacrament of penance or reconciliation he pronounces absolution in the name of Christ. But it is above all in presiding at the eucharist that the bishop or presbyter exercises his priesthood, for there (to quote again the words of the Anglican-Roman Catholic statement) he 'in reciting again the words of Christ at the Last Supper and distributing to the assembly the holy gifts is seen to stand in a sacramental relation to what Christ himself did in offering his own sacrifice'.[8]

Are these priestly functions then characteristic of the ordained ministry, so that here we can find its *differentia* from the general ministry of the whole church? Even at this point one must return a qualified answer. The bishop or presbyter is the normal minister of the sacraments mentioned. However, as is well known, in an emergency a lay person may baptize, and in some parishes deacons regularly baptize. A lay person may also hear a confession and give assurance of forgiveness. It is sometimes claimed that in the absence of a priest a lay person might preside at the eucharist, and there is no indubitable evidence that this may not have happened in the early days of the church when forms of ministry were still fluid. One obviously cannot legislate for extraordinary and abnormal situations or say what it would be right for a group of lay people to do if they found themselves washed up on a desert island. But what one can say about any appeal to an apparent lack of order or diversity of order in the early church or in some parts of it is that it was a temporary and apparently unsatisfactory state of affairs which soon gave way to a more orderly situation in which the mysteries of the sacraments were safeguarded by entrusting them to duly commissioned officers of the Church. As Piet Fransen once said, 'Without the priesthood, prophetism is doomed to anarchy. . . The institution and the charism are not mutually exclusive, but sustain each other.'[9] The church which Paul knew at Corinth is surely more of a warning than an example to subsequent generations of Christians.

Though presidency at the eucharist is the function which most fully and clearly expresses the distinctive priesthood of the ordained ministry, we should remember that this function has its setting in the whole constellation of functions outlined above, and that these in turn are to be seen in the context of the church. They provide an exciting mansize (or womansize?) job important both to church and world, so that the Christian minister has no need to imitate other rules rather than perform those that belong to Christian ministry. But the ministry is not just a matter of role or job or function. From our consideration of ministerial functions, we must go on to take up the question of ministerial character.

(ii) Ministerial character

We live in the age of functional man. That is to say, a man or woman is considered in terms of what he or she does. A man is a train driver or a bank clerk or whatever it may be. Of course, no one is a train driver or a bank clerk for all the time. But then we speak of roles, and this word, too, carries connotations of the external and the superficial. When the bank clerk comes home at night, he lays aside his working role and takes up the roles of husband and father. What we seem afraid to do is ever to come to the person himself, the person who remains in some sense identical through the many functions and roles, the person who not only *does* things but *is* someone. Perhaps indeed we have come to doubt whether there is a personal reality, and believe that there is nothing but the sum or aggregate of changing functions and roles. Gabriel Marcel, one of the most severe critics of the 'functional man' idea, has claimed that one of the diseases of modern man is his loss of ontological sense. He has become so absorbed in what he does that he no longer has any sense of who he is.

One does not wish to deny that there is a considerable element of truth in the idea of functional man. Being and doing are closely related. It is through our deeds and decisions that we become persons, and what we do makes us who we are. But the human reality is not exhausted by the functions which any individual performs. Also, as time goes on and we develop our characters, what we are begins to determine what we do. This is surely true of the Christian minister. We can list his various roles and functions – he is servant, proclaimer, priest; he preaches, baptizes, presides at the eucharist, and so on. But does it make sense to ask, *who* is it that does these things or appears in these roles? What kind of *person* do we meet here? I think it does make sense to ask such questions. Daniel Day Williams made the essential point in his little book on ministry when he wrote: 'Vocation is more than a role; it is a life dedicated and a responsibility assumed. No one should be playing a role at the point where ultimate things are at stake.'[10]

If ministry were merely a role or a function or a collection of functions, then there might seem to be no need for a distinctive ordained ministry in the church. The church would consist, so to speak, of modular Christians, any one of whom might, perhaps at a moment's notice, be fitted into any appropriate functional slot. Certainly, everyone recognizes that many functions need training and preparation. Even a seasoned preacher would hardly feel comfortable if he had to give a sermon at five minutes' notice. But is presidency at the eucharist, for instance, merely performing the function of reciting certain words and doing certain ceremonial acts, so that anyone who is literate and has had a little practice could do it as well as anyone else? Or is there more to it? Is there a deeper connection between ministry and presiding at the eucharist than can be expressed by words like 'role' and 'function'? Or again, can this particular function be separated and performed in isolation from that whole constellation of functions which form the work of an ordained minister?

Like Daniel Day Williams, I think there is more to ministry than role and function. The matter is expressed more fully by R. C. Moberly in his classic book, *Ministerial Priesthood*.

There are not only priestly functions or priestly prerogatives; there is also a priestly spirit and a priestly heart – more vital to true reality of priesthood than any mere performance of priestly functions. Now this priestly spirit is not the exclusive possession of the ordained ministry; it is the spirit of the priestly church. But those who are ordained 'priests' are bound to be eminently leaders and representatives of this priestliness of spirit, and they have assigned to them an external sphere and professional duties which constitute a special opportunity, and a charisma of grace which constitutes a special call and a special capacity for its exercise. Such opportunity and call are inseparable from the oversight of the Christian body to Godward, and they are as wide as is the life of the Christian body. Leadership in eucharistic worship, truly understood, is its highest typical expression, the mystical culmination of its executive privilege; but eucharistic leadership, truly understood, involves many corollaries of spirit and life.[11]

Needless to say, I do not mean, and Moberly did not mean, that the ordained minister is better or more inward or more spiritual than his lay brothers and sisters. But within the order and economy of the church, he is distinct, for he has received a special call, has taken on a special responsibility, and has been given in ordination a special grace to strengthen him. When we remember that ministry is a gift, a grace bestowed by Christ, then we shall be in no danger of thinking that the ordained ministry is a superior caste in the church. The ordained ministry owes everything it has to Christ – it is indeed *his* ministry embodied in a special way. This is recognized by the church's teaching that the validity of a sacrament does not depend on the personal worthiness of the minister of the sacrament. Christ is himself the true minister and agent in the sacraments, and the unworthiness of the human representative cannot block Christ's bestowal of grace. But this was never intended to suggest that the minister's worthiness or unworthiness is a matter of indifference! Priesthood is not content with bare validity but seeks to be effectual in enabling the recipient of the sacrament to *be*, and this implies that the priest himself must not only *do* the priestly act but *be* a priest in the closest communion with the great High Priest, Jesus Christ.

The traditional word used by theologians to designate the peculiar being or status of the ordained minister, that which underlies and unites his various roles and functions, finding expression in them, is the word 'character'. This is not a popular word at the present time. To those whose ways of thinking are pragmatic, empirical and analytic, the idea of character may seem just a mystification. They feel safer when dealing with functional man. But functional man is depersonalized man, and his functions may eventually be taken over by machines without any difference in efficiency, or even with increased efficiency. With a little imagination, one could even visualize the advent of the machine in ministry! But it would be in this matter of priesthood and the care of souls that the inadequacy of any merely functional view would be exposed. The notion of character is meant to supply what is lacking in a functional account of ministry.

I do not deny that the traditional doctrine of priestly character was expressed in scholastic philosophical categories which nowadays we judge to be too rigid and impersonal for describing the kind of phenomenon which is here in question. To some extent, this may excuse the impatience of some modern writers on ministry. Anthony Harvey, for instance, brusquely dismisses the idea of character as something that can find no place in his account of ministry.[12] But what is required is to re-examine the idea of character to find out what was of value in it and what it had to say that the functional account leaves out. The contemporary theologian does not have to dismiss the idea of character as foundational to ministry, for he has at his disposal more personal and more up-to-date categories in which to express the abiding value of the idea of priestly character, and most of the remainder of this chapter will be devoted to rehabilitating the idea of character, especially by attempting to throw light on the theological sense of 'character' by a comparison with the closely related use of the term in ethics.

In its literal sense, the Greek word *charakter* signified the distinctive mark made by a seal, die, or similar instrument. The word is used only once in the New Testament, in the Epistle to the Hebrews, where Jesus Christ is said to be the 'express image of [God's] person' or, alternatively translated, the 'very stamp of his nature' (Heb. 1.3). In modern usage, the word 'character' has developed a great many senses, but, as indicated above, we shall take our clues chiefly from ethical usage. I would like to say that in doing this I shall be largely following the analysis offered by Stanley Hauerwas in his splendid study of theological ethics entitled *Character and the Christian Life*.

The parallel between ethical and theological conceptions of character emerges right away, because, just as we have seen that there are two views of ministry standing in some tension, the functional view expressing itself in terms of roles and performance, and what may be called the onto-logical view concerned with who or what the minister is, so there have been for long two types of ethical theory, the one understanding morality chiefly in terms of commands, actions and overt behaviour, the other understanding the moral life more in terms of virtue and the formation of moral persons and even moral communities. It is no accident that the morality of commands and acts has, in the specific area of Christian ethics, flourished chiefly among Protestants, while Catholic moralists have been concerned with the ethics of virtue. Likewise Protestants have been inclined to view ministry in a functional way. In the forthright words of Luther (though I think Calvin and many later Lutherans would disagree), 'Whoever comes out of the water of baptism can boast that he is already a consecrated priest, bishop and pope, although of course it is not seemly that just anybody should exercise such an office . . . but a priest in Christendom is nothing but an office-holder.'[13] On the other hand, Catholic thinking has been dominated by such ideas as priestly formation and priestly character. But although these two views have often been in tension, my own belief is that both in ethics and theology they are complementary. The functional view in isolation is superficial and fails to do justice to the personal reality of a human being, but it is not cancelled out by the ontological view but is rather given depth and cohesion.

How then does a modern ethicist think of character? Clearly, character is not a thing, but is more like a pattern – a pattern that can be traced in a person's behaviour and that shows elements of directionality and consistency. 'The clearest example of character,' writes Stanley Hauerwas, 'is one in which a life is dominated by one all-consuming purpose or direction.'[14] This, however, would be the extreme case, and there can be examples of strong character in lives where there is a diversity of purposes and interests, provided that these are so ordered as to be brought into a unity. This, in turn, is effected by having an overarching interest or purpose, an 'ultimate concern', if we may borrow Tillich's expression. Proximate concerns are subordinated to the ultimate concern which gives, as it were, a definite set to the person's policies. But character is not just an adjective of policy. On the contrary, character produces some actions rather than others, for it is constituted by the priorities and value-judgements of the person in question. Indeed, character is scarcely distinguishable from the person himself.

It is perfectly clear from the way I have been describing it that character is not something that can be acquired in a moment. Character needs formation, and this may require quite a long time. Once character has been formed, then it does introduce a pattern of stability and reliability into life, but this does not mean that now there is an end to growth. Character needs to be exercised, and it deepens and develops with exercise and experience. It is not an *idée fixe*, still less a defence-mechanism that builds up routine ways of acting. But it does provide a way of approaching the new and unfamiliar so as to learn the possibilities concealed in them, and as these possibilities are learned, character itself takes on new dimensions.

Where does character come from? Obviously it has several

sources. There is first the given genetic inheritance of every individual, the innate propensities, capacities, weaknesses. These constitute, so to speak, the raw material of character. Within limits, they determine what it is possible for one to become. Yet this raw material is plastic and malleable, and there are many possibilities within it. Next, there is everything that works on a person from outside. There are the accidents of one's own history and upbringing, and these may have good or bad influence. There is the impact of society and culture, and none of us can help absorbing many of the beliefs and value-judgments of the society in which we are placed. There is also the tremendously important factor of education, the systematic training of mind and spirit. These three influences that come from outside we may call the passive elements in the formation of character, for, along with the genetic material, they are part of the given situation of our lives. We have not chosen them, we cannot escape them and we have to come to terms with them. But there is also an active side to the formation of character. To some extent, each one of us chooses to be the kind of person that he or she is. We respond to ideas that appeal to us or we set up images of what we wish to become or we engage in hero-worship. In each case, we strive to realize an ideal self of our choosing. Finally, the Christian would want to add to the factors mentioned another one, divine grace. The Christian believes that the attainment of character is not just an accident of birth or environment or the fruit of unaided human struggle, but that there is a co-working of God in all this, coming through prayer, the sacraments and life in the Christian community, and that this opening to God is of the highest importance.

The foregoing remarks apply to character in general and are made from within the perspective of ethical theory. We have now to return to the theological context and to the specific question of ministerial or priestly character. What light is thrown on it by the matters discussed above?

We may conveniently attempt an answer to this question by considering in order the various steps by which one enters the ordained ministry. These can be seen as steps in the formation of a special type of character.

First, there is vocation, the calling of God. The ministry is a gift and a summons, not something that we have chosen for ourselves. When a priest is asked, 'What made you decide to enter the ministry?', he may very likely reply that he hardly knows. All he may be able to say is that at some time in his life he felt a calling. The call of God to the ordained ministry is a special case of election. To some extent, all Christians have known the meaning of election. It is that inner constraint, that claim of God, that fascination with Christ, which lays hold upon one and draws one on, perhaps at first unwillingly. It has its prototype in pre-Christian times in the summons to Abraham and to all the spiritual leaders of Israel who came after him. Usually anyone called to the ministry has already known this experience of election into the people of God. The calling to ministry is an extension of election, the summons to a new relationship. And already the experience of this calling has had its ontological consequence and has begun to shape the character of the person called, touching the very depth of that person's being. For no one who has known such a call can ever be quite the same again. Such a person cannot just settle down as if nothing important had happened, but from now on will be attentive to God's calling and let it be the guiding principle in life.

This brings us to the next point. God's calling elicits the human response, the consent and co-operation of the one who is called. We have seen that character is formed partly by what is simply given to us but partly also by our own active pursuit of an ideal, by our deliberate choice to seek to become one kind of person rather than another. This is true of ministerial character, as well as of character in general. It requires the dedication and self-giving of one who is called to ministry. We have seen, too, that character is formed where there is one over-riding interest in a person's life, or where at least the diverse interests of that person's life are ordered in subjection to an ultimate concern. The coming of God's kingdom in the world and the service of that kingdom become the focus of the minister's interest and endeavour, and give the distinctive shape to ministerial character. There is also the negative side. To choose one thing inevitably implies the renouncing of other things. The ordination vows speak not only of what is to be chosen and done, but also of 'laying aside the study of the world and the flesh'. Sacrifice is a necessary element in priestly character. In consenting to become this kind of person and consenting to let character be formed by the interests of the kingdom of God rather than any merely egotistical interest, the Christian minister must make some renunciations.

I have been careful to point out that the formation of character depends on having either one over-riding interest which excludes all others, or a hierarchy of interests in which one has an ultimate and directing role. This, of course, raises questions about ministry. Some have believed that dedication to God's service and the pursuit of the kind of character which this demands call for a total renunciation of other interests, and so they have, for instance, advocated celibacy or even a total shunning of secular culture and the affairs of the world. The church will always need some single-minded ministers, and I shall return to the point shortly. But others believe that different life-styles are possible in the ministry and that other than directly religious pursuits can have their place even in a life dedicated to the service of God. They believe that ministerial character can be formed and can be effective in ways that may touch a broader segment of life, even if there is not the intensity of a total dedication. One has to notice also that 'total dedication' brings with it the dangers of narrowness, lack of touch with everyday human problems and even a touch of fanaticism.

These questions take on a new importance nowadays because of the shortage in some countries of vocations to the ministry and the economic difficulties of many churches in supporting full-time clergy, even when they are available. Thus there is a demand for auxiliary ministers, worker priests, or whatever they may be called – those who would support themselves by earning a living in a secular occupation but would also be ordained and act as priests of the church. It is sometimes questioned whether 'part-time ministers' (if that is a permissible expression) can really have priestly character or whether they would be like the 'mass priests' of a former time, so that ministry would have been reduced to a purely functional concept. I myself think that it is possible for ministry and ministerial character to be conjoined with a secular occupation, provided always that the ultimate concern of such a minister is with the Kingdom of God. Let us acknowledge, however, that it makes a very heavy demand on the person who offers himself for this work. But it is probable that this type of ministry was common in the early days of the church, and we have to be careful not to confuse the theological reality of ministry and priestly character with the sociological accident that in Western countries we have for a very long time been accustomed to full-time salaried professional clergy. In any case, full-time occupation is no guarantee of dedication or of the presence of priestly character. In eighteenth-century England there were plenty of 'full-time' bishops and clergy who were in practice very much 'part-timers', rarely in their sees and parishes, and giving little outward sign that the kingdom of God was the focus of their hopes and affections.

Priesthood is a lifelong commitment and a lifelong vocation, and indeed it takes the best part of a lifetime for the full flowering of priestly character. We live in a time when many are unwilling to make lifelong commitments, whether in vocation or in marriage or in other ways. I do not myself believe in 'temporary ordinations' – these would be possible only on an extreme functional view of ministry, and are impossible on the deeper conception which I am trying to expound and which, one may safely say, is in accordance with the traditional teaching of the church. But what is possible is a temporary commitment to particular forms or styles of ministry, and this is an idea worth considering. For instance, I did say earlier that the church will always need some people who dedicate themselves with an exclusive intensity. Surely there are in the churches today young clergy at the outset of their careers who might be willing to promise that for five years, let us say, they would not marry, they would live on a minimal allowance, and they would serve in whatever place the church authorities decided that they were needed. Such a corps of young clergy, utterly dedicated, could become as it were the 'shock troops' of the church and they might accomplish much in the way of mission and renewal. At the end of the five years, some might wish to continue in this style of ministry, others might decide to take up more conventional forms.

I have spoken of vocation to the ministry and willing response, but these things do not happen just between an individual and God. They take place in the context of the church, and it is the church which tests the calling of the individual, judges his fitness and the sincerity of his response, and then provides the training and formation that he needs. It is this period of formation that is of vital importance to the making of the priest and the building of priestly character. This cannot be the work of a moment, any more than is the case with moral character. Priestly character is certainly ontological, but is in no sense magical. The questions of ministerial training and priestly formation are vast, and they need not be the same for all, for variety is desirable within the ministry and we are coming better to recognize that ministry is better done in teams where there is a pooling of special gifts and aptitudes than by one person trying to do everything. Nevertheless, some things are necessary to all forms of ministry, and some balance must be kept as between intellectual and practical, contemplative and active, pastoral and missionary, and all the other aspects of ministry. However variable the forms of ministry, there is a recognizable priestly character running through them all, formed by devotion to God and his Kingdom, openness and availability to others, an inward strength of spirit.

If it seems that I am now presenting an impossible picture of ministry, let me move on to the next step. Vocation, response, formation in and by the church are followed by ordination. The various rites of ordination sum up and recapitulate the steps that have gone before. But something new is added, the sacramental dimension, which is God's commitment to his ministers, his promise of a grace and charism to sustain them in their impossible vocation. This is the deepest formative factor of all in the making of priestly character – the relation to God. And though priests sin like other human beings, God keeps recalling them to their vocation, electing them again to be leaders among his people.

Of course, ordination is not the end of the story. Although it is the climactic moment in the making of a minister, character does not fall ready made from heaven at that time or at any other. Character continues to deepen and develop as it is exercised and as it encounters new situations. As the development goes on and the human life is more and more penetrated by the divine life, we begin to understand what theologians have meant by the 'indelibility' of priestly character. An irreversible process has been set going and it will continue through this life and, we may suppose, beyond. To be sure, the process is sometimes arrested, the character is sometimes not exercised, human beings through sin fall away from and even renounce their commitments and solemn vows. But God remains faithful in his commitment and what he has done can never be quite undone. Karl Barth makes a startling suggestion that is well worth pondering: that even Judas could not entirely renounce the apostolic commission he had received from Christ, for 'his election excels and outshines and controls his rejection'.[15]

I have stressed ministerial or priestly character as a distinctive gift for those who are called to a distinctive ministry in the church, but finally I want to come back to the point that all this belongs within the context of the whole church. The distinctive ministries may be distinctive, but they are closely integrated into the general ministry of the church. I have indicated that calling to the ordained ministry is a special kind of election and continuous with the election of all the faithful. Similarly, the ministerial character is a special development of the character which originates in baptism. There is distinction without separation within the indivisible body of Christ. And the end of it all is sanctification, the making of a holy people who can share in the life of God.

16

The Bishop and the Theologian

Ideally, the bishop and the theologian ought to be one and the same person. At least, this is what one is tempted to say. However, when we remember that, ideally, the bishop ought also to be pastor, administrator, fund raiser, representative of the church in public life, and so on . . . and when we remember further that this is not an ideal world, then perhaps we must accept that usually the bishop and the theologian will be different persons. Still, one would like to think that the bishop, if not a theologian in the sense of one who teaches or writes theology, would be at least a theologically minded person, and that among the many qualities demanded of a bishop, sound theological learning and the habit of thinking theologically would rate very high. For when we consider the decline in the churches today, I think David Edwards is correct in saying that 'the basic problem confronting the churches is unbelief'.[1] Or it may be that one should say 'lack of belief' rather than 'unbelief', by which I mean that there is ignorance and bewilderment concerning Christian belief as much as straight rejection of it. In any case, there is a crying need for theology, if that means elucidating Christian faith in terms that are understandable to the modern world and designed to make contact with its ways of thinking. It is for this reason that theology ought to get a much higher rating in the church than it usually does, and it is for this reason too that any bishop who hopes to give leadership to his flock in these days must be theologically informed.

I was careful to say at the beginning of this essay that one is *tempted* to believe that the bishop and theologian ought to be one and the same person. But theology is so dialectical and dialogical in character that it is probably better that the bishop and the theologian should be different persons. Yet to say this is to assume that the bishop is theologically minded, the theologian is pastorally concerned, and that the two of them are in regular dialogue with each other. I doubt whether this is the case in many dioceses.

In earlier centuries, bishops often were themselves the leading theologians of the church. Perhaps they were not so harassed with other matters in those days, though this is by no means certain. One thinks of men like Irenaeus, Athanasius, Augustine and many others. Admittedly, the great episcopal theologians accounted for only a handful of all the bishops at any given time. But there was a clear recognition of the bishop's close concern with theology. His seat was still more the chair of a teacher than the throne of a ruler. His responsibility was to hand on the faith and to maintain Christian truth. Yet we need not suppose that this was conceived as something utterly static and unchanging. New questions were always arising and had to be settled. From the beginning, there was a twofold mode of succession – succession in the doctrine received from the apostles, and the personal succession of the bishops as the chief teachers of the church. This twofold mode ensured both stability and development in the understanding of the Christian faith.

I mentioned that only a small number of bishops were great theologians even in the early centuries, and we must not imagine that there ever was a time when all bishops were also creative theological thinkers. From a very early time there were theologians who were not bishops and who were sometimes consulted by bishops. According to Eusebius, when Origen took up his residence in Caesarea about the year 217, 'he was requested by the bishops to expound the sacred scriptures publicly in the church, although he had not yet received the priesthood by the imposition of hands'. Some seem to have believed that 'this was never before either heard or done, that laymen should deliver discourses in the presence of the bishops'. But others claimed that there had been precedents.[2] A little further on in Eusebius we read that Firmilianus, bishop of the Cappadocian Caesarea, 'was so favourably disposed towards Origen that he then called him to the regions in which he dwelt, to benefit the churches; at another time he went to visit him in Judaea and passed some time with him there for the sake of improvement in things divine. Moreover, Alexander, bishop of Jerusalem, and Theoctistus, bishop of Caesarea, attending him the whole time nearly like pupils their master, allowed him alone to perform the duties of expounding the sacred scriptures and other matters that pertain to the doctrines of the church.'³ So there were precedents for bishops taking counsel of theologians long before the days of Vatican II and Lambeth X!

The position today, of course, is vastly different from what it was in the early centuries. It is truly remarkable, in view of all the pressures upon them, that some bishops and even archbishops have been able to keep abreast of theological developments and make their own contributions to the debate. Perhaps they do show that it is possible even for a twentieth-century bishop to arrange his priorities in such a way that theology is not crowded out or kept far down the list because of the demands of administration and the like. However, it is perhaps only in exceptional cases that the bishop can remain as a creative theologian, and more frequently his theological reflection will take place in dialogue with full-time theologians acting as advisers.

But here we strike on another difficulty. We hear much about the divorce nowadays between theology and the life of the church. This is in part due to the fact that bishops and parish priests are so overwhelmed with a multitude of duties that they have little time left for theological reading and reflection. But many of them would lay the blame on the theologians, and say that they are not dealing with questions that are germane to the life of the church and that they are frankly unhelpful.

I do not believe we should talk of blame in these matters or try to apportion responsibility. The divorce does exist, but it is due in the main to changed social conditions. We have already noted how the bishop is under demands that keep him from theologizing, but we have also to consider sympathetically the situation of the modern theologian. The theologian today is caught up in the academic life of the universities. Theology is often suspect in university circles. What place is there for theological studies in a secular society? Is not theology a survival from pre-Enlightenment times? The young theologian especially may be very much aware of the apparently marginal position of his subject, and he may feel that the pressure is on him to establish its intellectual respectability, so to speak. All young academics are under pressure to do research and to publish contributions to their subjects. The theologian may feel that to maintain his position in the academic community, he has to devote his inquiries to strictly academic questions, and to eschew issues that might seem to be 'apologetic' or even 'propagandist'. So, for instance, he may devote himself to some fairly narrow historical inquiry, and may in consequence seem to have little to say about the significance of Christian faith for the contemporary world.

Since he is an academic as well as a churchman, the theologian sometimes experiences a tension. Even if he is a committed churchman, he is also jealous of academic freedom, and would be resistant to any attempt by the bishop or the church authorities to persuade him to produce theological reasons for pursuing a course of action that the church authorities considered desirable. To give an example of what I have in mind, I have known of theologians being put under pressure to find good theological reasons for certain ecumenical policies, and I could give other examples. Such pressure is utterly destructive of theological integrity, and ought to be resisted. It is quite another matter to ask theologians to investigate with an open mind questions that are of special interest to the church at any given time.

But just as I have suggested that bishops might order their priorities in such a way as to give a proper place to theological reflection, so I think it is not unfair to ask theologians, whatever the pressures upon them in the academic context, to hold themselves open and available as far as possible to the church. Many of them do in fact serve on commissions and committees, lecture at diocesan conferences or at institutes of theology for clergy and laity, and so on. When this occurs, I think the gap between theology and the life of the church often turns out to be narrower than has been supposed. Churchmen cannot get along without theology and theologians can scarcely be good interpreters of the Christian faith unless they have a living relation to the community of faith. The precise relation of the theologian to the church is a matter for debate among theologians themselves. Some would stress the independence of the theologian, his obligation to pursue truth as he sees it, and his vocation within the church as one who has to open up new understandings of faith in changing situations. Others would place more weight on the theologian's obligations towards the tradition, and would insist that even when he wants to lead the church into new ways of thinking, he must have regard to the peace of the church and always act in charity towards his fellow Christians. Again, some theologians lay stress on reason and experience as determining factors in their theological work. Others give more weight to the Bible and tradition. But I think that these differences are differences of emphasis rather than quite different ways of conceiving the work of the theologian or his relation to the church. I should think that almost all theologians recognize that there is a difference between the theologian and the philosopher of religion, or between a faculty of Christian theology and a department of religious studies. Theology comes out of a tradition and a community, while philosophy of religion is a more detached study of religion in general. Even the philosopher of religion, however, probably needs to have some measure of participation in religion if he is to bring any illumination to the subject.

At the present time, all human knowledge is undergoing rapid change, and this is bound to affect theology. There is no single theology today which enjoys undisputed authority among Christians. Even in the earlier part of the twentieth century, the theology of the Word of God, with Karl Barth as its principal architect, had a dominant place among the Protestant churches and in the ecumenical movement (though perhaps relatively few Anglicans were followers of Barth). On the Roman Catholic side, the revival of neo-Thomism, begun in the nineteenth century, came to its flowering in such notable figures as Jacques Maritain and Etienne Gilson. But these syntheses have fallen apart. Even Roman Catholic theology nowadays is infinitely varied. Karl Rahner writes of 'a number of theologies juxtaposed in a pluralist way, not contradicting each other, of course, but not susceptible of being positively incorporated into a higher synthesis'.[4] If indeed theology is an attempt to reflect on the unfathomable mystery of God as we have known him in Jesus Christ, then it would seem that multiplicity in theology is inevitable, for no single theology will ever grasp the mystery in its fullness.

This is not to say that everything is permitted or even that one theology is as good as another. But it does acknowledge the need for theological exploration and discussion. The truth of theology is dynamic and growing, and it is reached rather in the dialogue between different partial insights into the truth than in the construction of a 'consensus' theology, for this already threatens to become a theology that is dead and incapable of further development.

Can we now try to define more precisely the roles which bishops and theologians might play and how they might be related in the theological enterprise of the church?

Traditionally, the role of the bishop has been seen in conservative terms. His duty has been understood as that of maintaining the faith received from the apostles, of safeguarding it against errors, and of driving away strange doctrine. It must be confessed that this picture seems somewhat repressive in modern times! If indeed theology is in process of change and development, and if the bishop has a special responsibility in this area, can he discharge that responsibility simply by conserving a supposed deposit of truth? Should he not himself be a leader in theological exploration?

It is not easy to give a simple answer to these questions. I served on an advisory committee of the American Church under the chairmanship of the late Bishop Stephen Bayne

when we were asked to discuss the whole question of theological freedom and responsibility in the church. On the role
of the bishop, we agreed on the following wording: 'The
bishops' role is the calm enabling of the theological dialogue.
They themselves need not phrase experimental formulations, though if they are theologically competent and
phrase them in an expressedly experimental fashion, they
need not refrain. However, the bishops' principal role would
be to encourage inquiry.'[5] I would still find myself very much
in agreement with this. It is not saying that the bishops' role
should be a purely conservative one – on the contrary, the
bishops are to enable and encourage theological discussion.
But they themselves should be cautious of embracing startling innovations. They have a pastoral responsibility to all
their people, and they must try to carry all their people with
them. We know how at the present time some churches have
been grieviously divided between so-called 'conservatives'
and so-called 'progressives' – though these labels are tenden-
tious and question-begging. I have said already that conflict
and dialogue are necessary on the way to theological truth,
but the sad thing is that such conflict very often leads into
bitterness, division and polarization. The bishop will no
doubt have his own honest opinion on such divisive questions, but he must not be partisan and must try to prevent
polarization.

What are we to say of the role of the theologian? He can
be adventurous and innovative in ways that are difficult
for the bishop. Yet this always brings a certain temptation.
Theologians can only too easily begin to think of themselves
as the *teleioi*, those who have attained to a *gnosis* that is
beyond the reach of the ordinary faithful. Theologians sometimes refer, almost with contempt, to 'popular religion' or
'unreflecting Christianity'. In Germany, where perhaps theological professors have been more venerated than anywhere
else in the world, the complaint has sometimes been made
that the churches there suffer from a 'papacy of the scholars'.
This is certainly a danger, if academic theology is set over
against the religion of the ordinary people. But surely the
perception of spiritual truth is not a purely intellectual

matter. The fundamental truth of Christianity itself is the truth of Jesus Christ, and this truth exists concretely in his person before it is ever transcribed into theological propositions. It needs not intellectual acumen but spiritual sensitivity to apprehend it, and a truth may be implicitly grasped on the level of prayer and worship before it becomes theologically explicit. The *lex orandi* may give direction to the *lex credendi*.

Christian theology is too important a matter to be left to the professional theologians alone. The bishops cannot do it alone, but neither can the theologians. Yet I would want to say that the enterprise needs more than even bishops and theologians working together. It needs priests and people as well. Theology is a responsibility of the whole church, and can only be rightly done if the whole church participates.

Now, I am not saying this in the name of some foolish egalitarianism, as if all Christians were equally qualified to 'do theology', or as if questions of theology could be settled by majority vote. (On the last point, I would agree with Hans Urs von Balthasar that 'in a church which is essentially the little flock, it is not the majority which is right; it never has been, and today it is less so than ever'.[6]

It is not a case of everybody doing the same thing, but of each individual and each group bringing a particular *expertise* for a complex task, the successful performance of which needs all their contributions. The theologian brings his *expertise*, which consists in scholarship, whether in biblical studies or the history of theology or in philosophical theology or whatever it may be. But this remains academic until the theologian is joined by the bishop and his priests, who bring their special knowledge of the problems facing the church in mission and the cure of souls. Yet I would suggest that it is necessary to bring in still a third group, the laity, who know better than theologians or clergy the state of play in the workaday secular world. Left to themselves, theologians and bishops may fall to discussing questions which are sadly out of touch with where people are living today.

This task of doing theology together I call 'co-theologizing',[7] and it is an essential part of the rediscovered collegiality of all Christians within the church. I can think of no task that is more urgent for the church today than such co-theologizing, thinking deeply together about the meaning and implications of Christian faith in the modern context. Bishops have a special responsibility for getting such thinking going, for they know the needs and mood of the church and must enable and guide the dialogue. Theologians have their responsibility of bringing the treasures of their learning out of the study to the service of the church. Both bishops and theologians need the wisdom and knowledge of the lay people if their thinking is to make an impact where it is needed.

17

The Ordination of Women
to the Priesthood

The question of the ordination of women to the priesthood (and presumably therefore also to the episcopate) is one that has been debated in the Anglican communion for a good many years. I do not intend to rehearse the arguments, for I think we are all familiar with them. I do want to say, however, that both sides have had distinguished advocates, both sides have adduced weighty considerations, both sides have argued the case with skill and integrity. Both sides then deserve respect, and the question cannot be held to have been conclusively settled one way or the other. In the Roman Catholic and Orthodox communions, the debate has hardly begun.

But in the Anglican communion, the question is no longer only an academic one about possibilities. Some branches of this communion have already proceeded to the ordination of women priests. Female presbyters exist, and even those who would deny the ontological reality of women priests are not able to deny their empirical actuality. This fact, that women priests exist, complicates the issue considerably, for some churches of the communion are still at the stage of discussing whether they are going to ordain women, others that have already ordained them are dealing with the problem of how most effectively to use their ministry, and a new set of problems arises concerning the relations between those churches that have women priests and those that do not.

Before going any further, it would be only fair if I were to tell you where I stand myself on some of these issues. On the main point, I have for many years accepted that there are no decisive theological objections against the ordination of women.[1] I prefer to put it in this negative way, for good theology, like good mathematics, prizes economy, and it is enough here simply to establish that there are no decisive barriers. I went further in expressing the hope that women would eventually be ordained, and I would have no problems myself about accepting the ministrations of a woman priest. But, on the other hand (and this may seem like typical Anglican compromise) I have also been consistent in maintaining that the ordination of women to the priesthood should wait until there has been reached a substantial consensus on the question. I do not think that a nineteen-hundred-year-old tradition can be overturned by a simple majority vote at a single session of the governing body of one part of the church. This makes our talk about collegiality very hollow. I was myself ordained in the American church, so I hope my American friends will bear with me as one who still cares very deeply for the church in the US when I say that I was most unhappy about the way in which that church has gone about the ordination of women. So much then for my own views on the matter.

But now I come back to the substantive problems. I have said that I do not intend to rehearse the familiar arguments for and against. Instead, I would like to do three things. First, to take a step back from the arguments, so to speak, to try to sort them into categories, and then subject the different categories to critical evaluation, asking what weight attaches to arguments in each category. Second, I want to explore a little further what we mean by 'consensus'. How much agreement must there be before such a major innovation as the ordination of women priests is implemented? Obviously these two points are of interest chiefly in those churches which have not yet decided whether to ordain women. But since women priests are already a fact, and one that is not going to go away, there is a third group of problems. How, given the fact that we are still far from a consensus and that opinion is deeply divided, do we arrange matters within individual churches, within the Anglican communion as a whole, and in Anglican relations with other communions?

First, then, there is the analysis and evaluation of arguments used at the stage when a national or regional church is still considering the pros and cons of the case. I would hope that churches which have still to decide will show themselves more critical of the arguments on both sides than did the churches which have already decided. Everyone, of course, wants to claim that his arguments are theological, and if one could clearly distinguish between theological and, let us say, practical and sociological considerations, then in any conflict the weight would lie on the theological side. But the trouble is that it is very difficult to make such neat distinctions. On the one hand, every theology comes out of a particular historical situation and is therefore culturally conditioned and to some extent influenced by an ideology.[2] This seems to me to put a question mark opposite many of the arguments which the defenders of a male priesthood draw from the New Testament, for instance, Paul's understanding of the husband as the head of the wife or the fact that Christ chose only males as his apostles, as if this implied some hidden theological judgment about the maleness of priesthood, or even the fact that Christ himself was male. On the last point, Christ's *humanity* has always been of first-class theological importance in the many struggles against docetism, but it is only in our journalistic epoch that people have begun probing into the *sexuality* of Jesus, and I find it hard to see how this has any more relevance to theological questions than the colour of his eyes or his bloodgroup. On the other hand (and this point is often overlooked because of the prevailing myth of 'value-free' science[3]) the sociological critique of theology needs itself to be criticized, though it very rarely is. If every theology bears the traces of an ideology, it is equally true that every sociology has its inbuilt theology or possibly atheology, that is to say, its implicit value system in the light of which it selects and evaluates its facts. The sociological critique of theology demands to be corrected by the theological critique of sociology. It is the sociologist Peter Berger himself who has pointed out that while it is easy for us to see the evidences of cultural conditioning in the New Testament or in traditional theology, we remain blissfully unaware of our own conditioning.[4] In the matter which we are presently considering it does seem to me that some of those who have been most forward in criticizing the tradition on the grounds of its cultural bias have themselves been operating in terms of an uncriticized secular ideology, characterized by egalitarianism, relativism, immanentism and sometimes too the alleged need for confrontation – characteristics which are all very questionable from a Christian point of view. I make these points to show that although some churches have already come to decisions on the question of women's ordination, the argument is by no means over and ought to be pursued in greater depth and with more critical acumen in those churches where no decision has yet been taken. Whatever decisions they may eventually reach, one would also hope that they would be expressed in a properly modest form, and with the explicit recognition that those who think otherwise have integrity also and their rightful place within the church.

Next, we come to the question of a consensus. This is a difficult idea to pin down. It cannot mean everyone thinking alike. Not only is that a state of affairs which will never come about; it would also mean the death of theology as a living exploration into truth. Theology is a dialectical science, so that every minority view, yes, even every heretical and schismatic view, has its elements of truth and justification, so that the majority view needs the constant stimulation and correction of the minority view if one is to move along the path that leads to deeper truth. A measure of pluralism is today a healthy and acceptable state of affairs in the churches, as in society at large. But sheer pluralism would mean the dissolution of the church. The liberty of pluralism is possible only where it is contained within wide areas of agreement. This is especially the case where we are concerned (as in the present instance) not only with belief but with practice as well, though belief and practice can never be quite separated. The ordination of women to the priesthood and the episcopate would be such a novel step that it does seem to demand a large measure of consensus if it is not to provoke very deep division or even schism. I should think that such a consensus could be understood as the two-thirds majority required in many bodies as a condition for making radical changes, and this majority should be realized severally among bishops, clergy and lay people. I believe also that when such a degree of consensus is reached, many of those who had previously opposed the change will accept that it represents the mind of the church, perhaps even the leading of the Holy Spirit, and will go along. But we must remember too that the church is not a political institution, and truth is not decided by majority votes.

In the two preceding paragraphs, I have obviously been thinking mainly of regional or national churches, and in the first instance, it is within such a grouping that consensus has to be obtained. But the question does arise whether, on such an important and potentially divisive issue as the ordination of women to the priesthood, one should not look for a wider consensus than that of the regional or national church. It is true, of course, that within the Anglican communion each constituent church is autonomous. But I must confess I am not much impressed with the idea of an autonomous national church. This is surely a cultural rather than a theological entity, and is especially anomalous in days when there is much talk of collegiality, partnership, conciliarity and the like. If these are not just empty words to be bandied about in ecclesiastical assemblies, if they stand for a real desire to share experience and decision-making, then each so-called autonomous church ought to be in constant consultation with its sister churches. On the particular matter under discussion, it would surely have been wise if national churches had deferred action until after the Lambeth Conference of 1978 when they would have been able to consult together and give some guidance in the name of the whole Anglican communion, following on the study and reflection recommended by the Lambeth Conference of ten years earlier.

Some people would even argue that the Anglican communion should not act without a consensus that includes Rome and the Orthodox, but this may be asking too much. If there is ever to be action on controversial questions, one can hardly wait for the whole church to come to a common mind. In any case, Rome has on several occasions set the example of acting unilaterally, without regard for the Orthodox or the Anglicans and even less for the great Protestant churches. But to have reached a consensus within Anglicanism, though it would have been difficult, was not impossible if there had been more patience. To reach a consensus now is going to be far harder.

That brings us to our third problem or group of problems – those arising out of the fact that in the Anglican communion some churches have exercised their autonomy (which was certainly their legal right) and have ordained women priests, so that within the communion (and it remains a communion) there are now churches that have them and churches that don't; there are even churches which have them in some dioceses while other dioceses don't. Within the churches that have women priests there are some members who accept their ministrations and others who don't; in some areas schism has taken place while new questions are being raised about relations with Rome and the Orthodox. The consecration of women bishops (which is surely implicit in the ordination of women priests) adds a new dimension. How are these problems, some now actual, some still in the future, to be sorted out?

First of all, I think we have to get the problems into perspective. Although there are many difficulties in the idea, I think many theologians recognize that in Christianity there is what has come to be called a 'hierarchy of truths' that is to say, there are some doctrines which are central and comprise the very heart of Christian faith; there are others which are not so obviously central but which are nevertheless moderately important and well attested; while there are still others which are further from the centre and about

which there is some question as to whether they are clear
implicates of the central truths. It seems to me clear that the
question of whether women can be priests belongs within
this third outer area and that a difference of opinion ought
to be possible within one church. It is certainly not, I would
maintain, a question by which a church either stands or falls.
Hence I do not think that the ordination of women priests
in a church is a sufficient ground for people to leave that
church and set up a schismatic body, and I very much regret
that some have already done so. But there has rarely been a
schism in the history of the church when some measure of
blame did not lie on both sides. Have those who have left
us been sufficiently assured that their beliefs and consciences
would be protected and respected within a genuinely
comprehensive church? The Anglican communion has
always been a form of church that can accommodate wide
differences and today even the Roman Catholic church is
acknowledging that there can be a legitimate pluralism in
some areas where different theological opinions are possible.
Of course, in the past, while Anglicans may have disagreed
about doctrine, they have been fairly uniform in practice.
For instance, there have been different doctrines of the episcopate, but an invariable practice of episcopal ordination. In
the new situation, one may have to consider some pluralisms
of practice as well, in the functioning of women priests. Are
those members of the church who conscientiously believe
that a woman cannot validly consecrate the eucharist (and
who can prove beyond doubt that such persons are
mistaken?) to be forced either to go against their consciences
or to leave the church? Here I have in mind especially the
large number of bishops, clergy and lay people who are
unable to accept women priests but abhor the idea of schism
and loyally stay within the church, seeking a *modus vivendi*.
At the same time, we have equally to respect the consciences
of those bishops and others who believe it their duty to
recognize the genuineness of the call of certain women to
priestly ministry. Surely it is not impossible to work out a
way of living together in one church in a spirit of reasonableness and mutual respect, though it cannot be denied that

there will be awkwardnesses. And if this can be done within the church, one would hope that it can also be made clear to those who have left us that we want to be at one with them also, and that we believe that with God's help we can work out these problems within one family. Certainly, we should not be harsh or censorious toward so-called 'schismatics', but in anguish to be at one with them again.

Other problems may arise during the period (which may turn out to be a long one) when some Anglican churches have women priests and others do not. Here each church must respect and abide by the discipline of the other in the person of those of its members who from time to time may be guests in the other church, and if there is this reciprocal respect, the existing relation of full communion need not be disturbed.

Finally, there is also the question of how the existence of women priests in the Anglican communion will affect its relations with other communions. Many of the Protestant churches already have women ministers, so that it would make no difference in our relations with them. But I think we must note that most of these churches have a somewhat different view of ministry from that which is commonly held among Anglicans and is implicit in Anglican ordinals. It is not an accident that these Protestant churches do not use the word 'priests' for their ministers and that with them the sacramental and sacerdotal functions of ministry are less prominent. But the major difficulties will arise in the relations of Anglicans to Rome and the Orthodox, and some warning shots have already been fired. It will be sad indeed if the promising *rapprochement* between Rome and Canterbury is halted or slowed down by the ordination of women priests. This may very well happen, and I hope that Anglicans realize the price that may have to be paid for what is being done. But perhaps the coming together of Rome and Canterbury will not be blocked by the new developments, and here I would appeal to the generosity and understanding of our Roman Catholic friends in particular. If indeed, as I have claimed, women in the priesthood is a disputed question belonging to that area where pluralism is legitimate, is it not possible for the two communions to continue to grow together on the basis of the many things they have in common, while respecting differences of practice on matters which surely do not make or unmake a church?

18

Politics as Lay Ministry

A Lutheran pastor and theologian, Dietrich Bonhoeffer, has turned out to be one of the most influential figures in contemporary Christianity. He was one of the very few German churchmen who carried opposition to the Nazis to the length of joining the underground resistance movement and even of becoming involved in the unsuccessful attempt to assassinate Hitler. He was executed at thirty-nine years of age in the closing days of World War II. In a few years he had become world famous, not only as a Christian martyr but as the author of his posthumous *Letters and Papers from Prison*, expounding the vision of a modern Christianity that would be deeply involved in the affairs of the world.

There are many forms of Christian discipleship. Bonhoeffer chose political discipleship. Unfortunately, his theological reflections on the subject remained sketchy and incoherent, but it is important to remember that his motivation was genuinely theological. He had not abandoned religion for politics but remained to the end a devout believer who saw his Christian vocation within the political context.

Bonhoeffer has caught the imagination of so many contemporary Christians because his attraction to politics seems to chime in with much of the religious temper of our time. Christianity has become markedly more politicized in the past few decades (and there have been parallel developments in Islam and Buddhism). One has only to think of the increasingly political tone of pronouncements by the World Council of Churches, of the liberation theologies of South American Roman Catholics, or of the political clout wielded by conservative evangelicals in the United States. Religion and politics can never be kept entirely separate, but for better or worse religion is becoming increasingly politicized in our day.

Clearly, there are many reasons that could be cited to justify religious involvement in political affairs. Christianity (and presumably other religions as well) aim at the 'salvation' of human beings, and any idea of salvation must be comprehensive and touch on the whole of human life. Human beings need to be saved in their political as well as in their private dealings. We recognize more clearly today than perhaps people did in earlier times just how much structures and institutions go into the shaping of human lives so that it is hard to see how there could be any salvation or wholeness for individuals without a corresponding renovation of the social, political and economic structures in which their lives are set and with which they interact at innumerable points. Individual salvation, irrespective of socio-political considerations, would be possible only if that salvation were understood in purely other-worldly terms – really as an escape from this world rather than as a process which must at least begin in this world, even if its final consummation lies beyond. Christians have become more conscious of the need to relate the concept of salvation to our lives here and now. Partly this may be due to the Marxist criticism that religion has been so concerned with the hereafter that it has been indifferent to injustice in the here and now, partly it is due to the steady march of secularization which has affected even the religious understanding, but partly it has been due also to the recognition that if the creation is good, as Christian theology avers, then the created order is itself the theatre of salvation, a belief reinforced by the doctrine of incarnation. The created order in space and time may not be shunned as evil or regarded as simply a stage in the human pilgrimage to a spiritual goal, but deserves, as God's creation, to be treated with respect and moulded in all its dimensions, including the political one, toward the end of promoting wholeness or salvation among human beings.

But while all that is true, there is another side to the question. In most democratic societies there is nowadays separation of church and state. This may be written into the constitution, as in the United States, or it may just have developed gradually, as in England. While the Church of England remains established, the ties binding the church to the state have gradually been loosened. For instance, the church now has freedom in the ordering of its worship and a say in the appointment of its bishops. On the other hand, the state has in many matters such as divorce and abortion gone its own way in disregard of the church's teaching. Again, although twenty bishops still sit in the House of Lords, their political influence is negligible. On the whole, both church and state benefit from the distance that has been placed between them, so one must ask whether recent religious incursions into politics may not be putting the clock back.

It may be useful at this point to get some historical perspective on the question.

In the earliest days of Christianity, any direct political involvement by the church was out of the question. Christians existed as an alienated group on the fringes of society and were from time to time subject to persecution. Yet in these small Christian communities new kinds of human relationships were being established and old barriers between ethnic groups, the social classes and the sexes were being broken down. The Letter to the Ephesians in the New Testament gives us a fascinating glimpse of such a community. The church in those days was to society as a whole like a little leaven in the lump, but was not seeking to become the lump itself. Perhaps this is how it most effectively influences society – simply by showing that there is another and better way for human beings to live together. This may still be true. Perhaps it is in small and obscure congregations where the work of reconciliation is going on in the back streets of New York or Birmingham that we find the spearhead of the religious transformation of society, rather than in the noisy pressure groups protesting against whatever happens to be the current obsession of politically minded ecclesiastics or in the pretentious conferences and commissions which the churches set up.

When Constantine was converted to Christianity, a new relationship between the church and the Roman Empire came about. The once persecuted fringe had now become an ally of the state. The church historian of those days, Eusebius of Caesarea, has been called the first political theologian, and he did not hesitate to couple the names of God and Emperor: 'Now a bright and splendid day irradiated the churches. With choirs and hymns, they extolled first of all God, then they also celebrated the pious Emperor.'[1] While one can understand the sense of relief experienced by the Christians at that time, the day that Eusebius saw dawning was not going to be so bright as he expected. The close relation between church and state became the normal pattern in Europe for many centuries, both in the East and in the West. Cranmer, perhaps the chief architect of the post-Reformation Church of England, was as subservient to the state as ever Eusebius had been. A mainly sympathetic biographer has felt constrained to write: 'The phrase "God and the King" appears continually in Cranmer's letters, and it was indeed rare for him to write the name of the Almighty without bracketing it with that of Henry VIII.'[2] He also declares, 'There was hardly a page in the sacred scriptures which Cranmer and his colleagues were not prepared to pervert to the greater glory of King Henry.'[3] In Geneva, an equally close alliance of church and state took a different form. There the church dominated the civil authority, and Calvin's dictatorship in the city must be reckoned one of the most repressive in history, comparable only perhaps to the tyranny that prevailed in the Papal States before the liberation of Italy. On the whole, the story of the church's involvement in politics during many centuries of European history has been a depressing one. As a group, and with very few exceptions, ecclesiastics have shown themselves to be singularly inept or even dangerous in political matters. I shall mention some reasons for this in a moment.

But meanwhile, the picture presented has to be corrected by mentioning the achievements of laymen whose political endeavours were inspired by their Christian faith. To some extent, these lay people redeem the failures of the clergy. In

England, for instance, one would have to take account of the work of men like Lord Shaftesbury and William Wilberforce, men whose Christian vision was combined with parliamentary experience and a grasp of political realities, so that they were able to accomplish major advances in reducing social evils and improving the conditions of life for large numbers of their exploited contemporaries. These men got their original vision within the Christian congregation, which I have already described as the 'spearhead' of the religious transformation of society and seems to me far more important and effective than the ecclesiastical assembly with its solemn but frequently dubious pronouncements. In other words, a community of genuine vision and reconciliation, even if it is struggling for survival on the margin of society, is likely to be more effective than some high-powered commission.

We have noted that today we are living in a time when separation of church and state is regarded as desirable in most democratic countries. This is understandable, considering the many unhappy consequences that arose from the often unholy alliance of church and state in the past. Yet it hardly allows for the justifiable efforts of Christians (and adherents of other religions) to bring something of their vision of a renewed and reconciled society into the political processes of their time. Religion cannot and should not be kept altogether separate from politics, and those varied and confused attempts to introduce religious considerations into the political debate which we can see at the present time are a proof of this. But we have still to work out a new conception of the relations of church and state, to take the place of older conceptions that are no longer viable.

One guideline does seem to emerge from our reflections. If there is a political ministry of the church, it ought to be conceived as a lay ministry. Bishops and other clerics are politically too naive, for most of them have no first-hand acquaintance with industry or commerce or government. They suffer from the further weakness of cherishing ethical absolutes which they apply without regard to the relativities of particular situations. Finally, they are representative persons who cannot simply speak as individuals, and this means that they must avoid narrow partisan positions. That, I suppose, is why English law rightly debars priests from sitting in Parliament, and why the Pope has been actively discouraging his clergy from direct participation in political struggle. If the clergy do have a role in politics, it is not to leap into the arena themselves but to make their people sensitive to what enhances and what diminishes a truly human life. Where the principles of the Christian gospel are clearly taught and understood, this is bound to point us towards the humanization and even the Christianization of vast areas of society in which the law of the jungle still holds. But the practical policies designed to achieve such ends should be the work of lay people. The churches talk a lot about lay ministry, but usually think of it as a pale and rather amateurish imitation of the work of the ordained ministry – reading lessons or prayers or even preaching a sermon in church. The lay ministry is far more important than that, and lies in public life. A few active and intelligent lay Christians involved in the political process are worth a thousand sententious utterances by bishops and synods.

NOTES

Notes

1 Pilgrimage in Theology

1. F. H. Bradley, *Appearance and Reality*, Oxford University Press ²1897, p. 4.
2. J. Macquarrie, *An Existentialist Theology*, SCM Press 1955, p. 191.
3. Louis Bouyer, *Le métier de théologien*, Paris: Editions France-Empire 1979, p. 156.

This chapter first appeared as an article in *Epworth Review*, vol. VII, 1980. It has been slightly updated.

2 Theology and Ideology

1. Karl Popper, *Objective Knowledge*, Oxford University Press 1972, p. 146.
2. Michael Polanyi, *Personal Knowledge*, Routledge and Harper and Row 1964, p. 1.
3. Popper, op. cit., p. 266.

This chapter was originally a paper given at the Eleventh Downside Symposium and published in James Barnett (ed.) *Theology at 16+*, Epworth Press 1984.

3 The End of Empiricism?

1. G. Santayana, *Winds of Doctrine*, Harper 1957, p. 211.
2. See above, pp. 10f.
3. There is a fuller discussion of these questions in my book, *In Search of Humanity*, SCM Press and Crossroad Publishing Company 1982, ch. VI.
4. J. A. Martin, Jr, *Empirical Philosophies of Religion*, Columbia University Press 1945.
5. Ibid., p. 38.
6. Ibid., p. 80.
7. Ibid., p. 101.
8. Ibid., p. 102ff.
9. I. T. Ramsey, *Models for Divine Activity*, SCM Press 1973, p. 4.
10. Kai Nielsen, *Contemporary Critiques of Religion*, Macmillan 1971, p. 31.
11. A. Flew, in A. Flew and A. Macintyre (ed.), *New Essays in Philosophical Theology*, SCM Press 1955, p. 97.

This chapter in a slightly different form was first published in a special number of the *Union Seminary Quarterly Review*, Vol. XXXVII, 1981, honouring James A. Martin, Jr.

206   *Theology, Church and Ministry*

4 *Systematic Theology and Biblical Studies*

1. A. C. Thiselton, *The Two Horizons*, Paternoster Press and Eerdmans 1980, p. 307.
2. H-G. Gadamer, *Truth and Method*, ET Sheed & Ward 1975, p. 264.
3. Thiselton, op. cit., p. 57.

This chapter was first published in *Kairos*, no. 2, 1980.

5 *Tradition, Truth and Christology*

1. *The Documents of Vatican II*, ET ed. W. M. Abbott & J. Gallagher, Herder & Herder and Chapman 1966, p. 117.
2. *Sacramentum Mundi*, ed. K. Rahner et al, Herder & Herder 1968, vol. VI, p. 270.
3. Vincent of Lerins, *The Commonitory*, xxiii, 28.
4. *Documents*, p. 116.
5. B. Lonergan, *Insight*, Darton, Longman & Todd and American Library 1970, p. 246.
6. D. Wiederkehr, *Belief in Redemption*, ET SPCK 1979, p. 87.
7. Paul Tillich, *Systematic Theology*, Chicago University Press and Nisbet 1951–63; SCM Press 1978, Vol. II, p. 97.
8. K. Barth, *Church Dogmatics*, ET T. & T. Clark 1936–68, vol. 11/2, p. 484.
9. Don Cupitt, *Jesus and the Gospel of Love*, Lutterworth Press 1979, p. 21.
10. M. Heidegger, *Introduction to Metaphysics*, ET Yale University Press 1959, p. 155.
11. Immanuel Kant, *Critique of Judgment*, ET Oxford University Press 1952, pp. 99–100.
12. The Doctrine Commission of the Church of England, *Christian Believing*, SPCK 1976, p. 87.
13. John Knox, *The Church and the Reality of Christ*, Harper and Collins 1962, p. 29.

A Cardinal Heenan Memorial Lecture, first published in *The Heythrop Journal*, vol. XXI, 1980.

6 *The Anthropological Approach to Theology*

1. John Calvin, *Institutes of the Christian Religion*, ET James Clarke 1953, vol. I, p. 37.
2. F. D. E. Schleiermacher, *The Christian Faith*, ET T. & T. Clark 1928, p. 366.
3. B. Lonergan, *Method in Theology*, Darton, Longman & Todd 1971, p. 341.
4. M. Buber, *I and Thou*, ET T. & T. Clark ²1958, p. 75.
5. J. H. Newman, *Sermons bearing on Subjects of the Day*, 1869, p. 353.
6. R. C. Selby, *The Principle of Reserve*, Oxford University Press 1975, p. 22.
7. P. Berger, *A Rumour of Angels*, Doubleday and Penguin Books 1969, p. 66.
8. Immanuel Kant, *Critique of Practical Reason*, ET Macmillan 1929, p. 200.
9. Denys, *The Divine Names*, iv, 13.

10. G. Leibniz, *Monadology*, ET Oxford University Press 1898, p. 266.
11. K. Rahner, *Theological Investigations*, Vol. 1, ET Darton, Longman & Todd 1961, p. 184.
12. See above, p. 52.

A lecture delivered in honour of Dr Karl Rahner's eightieth birthday at Heythrop College in the presence of the *honorandus* on 17 February 1984. The appendix to this chapter contains a discussion with Dr Rahner after the lecture. First published in *The Heythrop Journal*, Vol. XXV, 1984.

7 God in Experience and Argument

1. Blaise Pascal, *Pensées*, Paris: Garnier-Flammarion 1973, p. 247.
2. Ibid., p. 136.
3. F. H. Bradley, *Appearance and Reality*, Oxford University Press ^{2}1897, pp. 5–6.
4. Martin Buber, *I and Thou*, ET T. & T. Clark ^{2}1958, p. 75.
5. As reported by J. R. H. Moorman, *A History of the Church in England*, A. & C. Black ^{3}1973, p. 298.
6. Pierre Teilhard de Chardin, *Hymn of the Universe*, ET Collins 1970, p. 24.
7. Martin Thornton, *My God*, Hodder & Stoughton 1974, p. 91.
8. See my essay, 'Feeling and Understanding', in *Studies in Christian Existentialism*, McGill University Press and SCM Press 1965, pp. 31–42.
9. James Richmond, *Theology and Metaphysics*, SCM Press 1970, p. 151.

This chapter was first published in the symposium *Experience, Reason and God*, ed. E. T. Long, Catholic University of America Press 1980.

8 The Idea of a Theology of Nature

1. A. Ritschl, *Justification and Reconciliation*, ET T. & T. Clark 1900, p. 29.
2. Ibid., p. 587.
3. When I use the word 'Nature' in what I call the 'broad inclusive sense', I shall capitalize it.
4. Harold K. Schilling, *The New Consciousness in Science and Religion*, United Church Press and SCM Press 1973, p. 225.
5. Barbara Ward and René Dubos, *Only One Earth*, Penguin Books 1972, p. 85.
6. D. D. Williams, 'Christianity and Naturalism,' *Union Seminary Quarterly Review*, Vol. XII, 1957, p. 47.
7. M. Heidegger, *Being and Time*, ET Harper and SCM Press 1962; Blackwell 1967, p. 75.
8. J. Habgood, *Truths in Tension*, Holt Rinehart & Winston 1964, p. 62.
9. See e.g. M. Heidegger, *Introduction to Metaphysics*, ET Yale University Press 1959, p. 13ff.
10. Ibid., p. 14.

This chapter was first published in a special number of the *Union Seminary Quarterly Review*, Vol. XXX, 1975, honouring the memory of Daniel Day Williams.

208   *Theology, Church and Ministry*

9   *The Anglican Theological Tradition*

1. *Documents of Vatican II*, ET. ed. W. M. Abbott & J. Gallagher, Herder & Herder and Chapman 1966, p. 356.
2. *Doctrine in the Church of England (1938)*, SPCK ²1982, p. 19.
3. Ibid., p. lx.
4. Ibid., p. 36.
5. S. W. Sykes, *The Integrity of Anglicanism*, Mowbray 1978, p. 47.
6. *Theological Freedom and Social Responsibility*, Seabury 1967, p. 32.
7. In his introduction to the new edition of the 1938 report, pp. lix–lx.
8. Ibid., p. lx.
9. *Believing in the Church*, SPCK 1981, p. 4.
10. Ibid., p. 9.
11. Ibid., p. 167.
12. Sykes, op. cit., p. 74.
13 *Christ, Faith and History*, ed. S. W. Sykes and J. P. Clayton, Cambridge University Press 1972.
14. Thomas Cranmer, *The True and Catholic Doctrine of the Sacrament of the Lord's Body and Blood*, Thyme 1907, p. 95.
15. John Jewel, *An Apology of the Church of England*, in *English Reformers*, ed. T. H. L. Parker, Library of Christian Classics, SCM Press and Westminster Press 1966, p. 29.
16. Quoted in J. R. H. Moorman, *A History of the Church in England*, A. & C. Black, ³1973, p. 234.
17. J. H. Newman, *Apologia pro Vita Sua*, Dent 1907, p. 133.
18. Quoted by G. Faber, *Oxford Apostles*, Faber 1933, p. 434.

Originally a lecture given at the Church of the Advent, Boston, on the occasion of the sesquicentennial of the Oxford Movement and first published in *The Anglican Tradition*, ed. Richard Holloway, Morehouse-Barlow 1984.

10   *Pride in the Church*

1. *The Times*, London, 17 November 1973.
2. Augustine, *City of God*, xiv, 3.
3. Reinhold Niebuhr, *The Nature and Destiny of Man*, Scribner 1941, Vol. I, p. 214.
4. Aristotle, *Nicomachean Ethics*, ii 23a.
5. G. W. F. Hegel, *The Phenomenology of Mind*, ET Allen & Unwin ²1931, pp. 229ff.
6. Jean Paul Sartre, *Being and Nothingness*, ET American Library 1956, pp. 361ff.
7. Peter Berger, 'A Call for Authority in the Christian Community', *The Christian Century*, 27 October 1971.

This chapter was first published in *Communio*, Vol. IV, 1977.

11   *The Idea of a People of God*

1. S. Kierkegaard, *Fear and Trembling*, ET Doubleday 1954, p. 75.
2. A. J. Heschel, *The Prophets*, Farrar Straus & Giroux 1962.

3. M. Arnold, *Literature and Dogma*, Smith, Elder & Co 1876, p. 31.

An inaugural lecture given at Tulane University, New Orleans, as the first
Visiting Professor of Judaeo-Christian Studies, 1980.

12 The Meeting of Religions in the Modern World: Opportunities and Dangers

1. H. Marcuse, *One Dimensional Man*, Sphere Books 1968, p. 14.
2. J. G. Davies, *Every Day God*, SCM Press 1973, p. 87.
3. Quoted by E. Conze, *Buddhism: Its Essence and Development*, Harper 1959, p. 157.
4. P. Berger, *A Rumour of Angels*, Doubleday and Penguin Books 1969, p. 94.

This chapter was first published as an article in *The Journal of Dharma*, Vol. I, 1975.

13 The One and the Many: Some Implications for Religion

1. S. Kierkegaard, *Repetition*, ET Harper 1964, p. 52.
2. S. Radhakrishnan, *Eastern Religions and Western Thought*, Oxford University Press 1959, pp. 127–8.
3. Plato, *Sophist*, 246A.
4. H. W. Richardson, *Toward an American Theology*, Harper 1967 (English Title *Theology for a New World*, SCM Press 1967), pp. 103ff.
5. J. Macquarrie, *Principles of Christian Theology*, Scribner and SCM Press ²1977, p. 198.
6. Raymond Pannikar, *The Trinity and World Religions*, Christian Literature Society, Madras 1970.
7. J. A. Dubois, *Hindu Manners, Customs and Ceremonies*, ET Oxford University Press ³1906, pp. 533ff.

This chapter was first published in the symposium *Meeting of Religions*, ed. Thomas A. Aykara, Dharmaram Publications, Bangalore 1978.

14 Commitment and Openness: The Christian and Other Faiths

1. Yasuo Furuya, 'The Significance of Asian Christianity: A Note to Western Theologians' in *Pacific Theological Review*, Vol. IX, 1977, p. 25.
2. Ibid., p. 26.
3. Karl Barth, *Church Dogmatics*, 1/2 ET T. & T. Clark 1956, p. 302.
4. Paul Tillich, *Systematic Theology*, Chicago University Press and Nisbet 1951–63; SCM Press 1978, Vol. I, p. 144.
5. Karl Rahner, *Foundations of Christian Faith*, ET Darton, Longman & Todd 1978, pp. 21, etc.
6. Hans Küng, *On Being a Christian*, ET Collins 1977, p. 103.
7. John Hick, *God and the Universe of Faiths*, Collins 1977, p. 102.
8. John Hick, *Death and Eternal Life*, Collins 1976, p. 29.
9. Ibid.
10. J. Macquarrie, *Principles of Christian Theology*, Scribner and SCM Press ²1977, p. 153.

11. H. R. Schlette, *Towards a Theology of Religions*, ET Herder & Herder 1966, p. 101.

12. W. E. Hocking, *Living Religions and a World Faith*, Allen & Unwin 1940, pp. 190–1.

13. Ibid., p. 201.

14. *Bhagavadgita*, Lesson the Fourth, 7–8.

This was the William Rossner Lecture delivered at Rockhurst College, Kansas City, in 1979 and first published in *Theology Digest*, Vol. XXVII, 1979.

15   The Church and the Ministry

1. H. Küng, *Why Priests?* ET Collins 1972, p. 53.

2. D. D. Williams, *The Minister and the Care of Souls*, Harper 1961, p. 11.

3. *Doctrine in the Church of England (1938)*, SPCK ²1982, p. 115.

4. ARCIC, *The Final Report*, SPCK 1982, p. 36.

5. W. M. Abbott & J. Gallagher, ed., *The Documents of Vatican II*, ET Herder & Herder and Chapman 1966, p. 27.

6. A. H. Baverstock, *Priesthood in Liturgy and Life*, Faith Press 1917, p. 25.

7. *The Final Report*, p. 35.

8. Ibid.

9. Piet Fransen, 'Orders and Ordination' in *Sacramentum Mundi*, ed. K. Rahner et al, Herder & Herder 1969, vol. IV, p. 307.

10. D. D. Williams, op. cit., p. 103.

11. R. C. Moberly, *Ministerial Priesthood*, John Murray 1910, p. 261.

12. A. E. Harvey, *Priest or President?* SPCK 1975, pp. 49–50.

13. Martin Luther, *Three Treatises*, ET Fortress Press 1982, p. 14.

14. S. Hauerwas, *Character and the Christian Life*, Trinity University Press 1975, p. 119.

15. Karl Barth, *Church Dogmatics*, 11/2, ET T. & T. Clark 1957, p. 504.

This chapter was first published as two articles in *The Expository Times*, Vol. LXXXVII, 1976.

16   The Bishop and the Theologian

1. D. L. Edwards, *The British Churches Turn to the Future*, SCM Press 1973, p. 3.

2. Eusebius, *Ecclesiastical History*, ET Bell 1903, p. 226.

3. Ibid., p. 233.

4. K. Rahner, *The Christian of the Future*, ET Herder & Herder 1967, p. 34.

5. *Theological Freedom and Social Responsibility*, Seabury Press 1967, p. 17.

6. Hans Urs von Balthasar, *Elucidations*, ET SPCK 1975, p. 95.

7. J. Macquarrie, *Principles of Christian Theology*, Scribner and SCM Press ²1977, p. 441.

This chapter was written as a preparatory paper for the Lambeth Conference of 1978 and was published in the volume of such papers entitled *Today's Church and Today's World*, CIO Publishing 1977. The book was specially concerned with the ministry of bishops.

17   *The Ordination of Women to the Priesthood*

1. I have already expressed this view in the first edition of *Principles of Christian Theology* in 1966, and have consistently maintained it.

2. See above, ch. 2, pp. 14ff.

3. See above, ibid.

4. P. Berger, *A Rumour of Angels*, Doubleday and Penguin Books 1969, p. 51.

This chapter was the introductory speech at a hearing on 'The Ordination of Women to the Priesthood' at the Lambeth Conference of 1978. An abridged version was published in *Report of the Lambeth Conference 1978*, CIO 1978.

18   *Politics as Lay Ministry*

1. Eusebius, *Ecclesiastical History*, ET Bell 1903, p. 419.

2. Jasper Ridley, *Thomas Cranmer*, Oxford University Press 1962, p. 257.

3. Ibid., p. 122.

This chapter was first published in *The Times Higher Education Supplement*, No. 529, 1982.